THE WRITER'S BRAINSTORMING TOOLKIT

THINKING IN NEW DIRECTIONS

PAM MCCUTCHEON

MICHAEL WAITE

PARKER
HAYDEN
MEDIA

DEDICATION

Pam would like to thank her critique group for taking the time to review the text and the members of Pikes Peak Romance Writers who graciously acted as guinea pigs and let us try out the concept on them. Special thanks, too, to Debra Dixon who provided the impetus for this idea with her character readings.

Michael thanks Pam and his wife, Sheri, for their diligence in bashing the mutant-freak ideas and rescuing the good ones that make up his contribution to this work. And thanks to Pam, for cooking up the concept for The Writer's Brainstorming Kit and inviting him along for the ride.

CONTENTS

INTRODUCTION

A recurring refrain in the writing business is that editors want fresh material—something different they haven't seen before. We'd all like to oblige them, but sometimes it's difficult to come up with a fully-fleshed, original concept when the only person available to brainstorm with is yourself.

Since we're all limited to one brain, we unfortunately fall into habits of characterization and plotting. Left to ourselves, we develop ruts of linear thinking and tend to respond in the same way to the same conditions (e.g., to the same basic plot lines). To break out of these ruts, we need outside input to trigger our thinking in new directions, to give our creativity something different and inspiring to play with.

Finding another person or three to share ideas with is one solution, but there are a couple of problems inherent in that. First, others aren't always available when inspiration or the creative urge strikes .. . and people have a tendency to be a bit peeved if you wake them at odd hours to listen to your latest brainchild.

Second, others have a tendency to become enamored with their own ideas—whether *you* find them useful or not—and veer off on unusable tangents. If they're writers, it might become even more difficult as they take fire from their own ideas and spin out scenarios that ignore your needs.

The ideal situation is to find a better way of brainstorming with yourself. That's what *The Writer's Brainstorming Kit* is all about—a way of using random concepts to trigger new associations in *your* mind, to break out of your conventional linear mode of thinking and take flight in new, unexpected directions.

So, give it a try. No matter whether you need help with getting started, creating a story from scratch, breaking through a block, adding depth to a character, or finding a new plot twist, shuffle the cards, and let them help you create something fresh and different.

WHAT YOU'LL NEED

The original print edition of *The Writer's Brainstorming Toolkit* came with a deck of fifty cards (hence the kit designation). That's rather expensive to print, so we added two cards to make it fifty-two. Now you can use a regular deck of playing cards to brainstorm with. Just draw a playing card, match it up with the card name below, and use that method to randomly select a card. Or . . . you could navigate to the table of contents that shows the pages with the card names, close your eyes, and stab your finger at random on the page. Whatever method you choose, get started brainstorming!

PART 1

HOW TO USE THE BOOK AND CARDS

1

UNDERSTANDING THE CARDS

In order to use this system, you first need to understand how it's laid out. There are fifty-two words (in alphabetical order) associated with the fifty-two cards in a regular deck of playing cards. These words are intended to trigger associations in your mind to add depth and interest to your story for a specific element of character or plot.

For example, if you need help in developing a character from scratch, you'll draw seven cards, one for each character category listed below. If you want to create a new plot, you'll draw five cards to correspond with each of the plot categories. Here's how the categories are set up:

CHARACTER CATEGORIES

Most of our character categories are derived from the method designed by Debra Dixon in her enlightening and useful book on characterization, *GMC: Goal, Motivation, and Conflict*.

As the late Paul Gillette used to say, a novel is a story about a likable or interesting character who overcomes seemingly insurmountable obstacles in search of a worthwhile goal. Ms. Dixon expands this to suggest that major characters should not only have meaningful goals, but should also have strong motivations for wanting those goals (which make the characters likable and the goals meaningful). And, of course, they must conflict—those seemingly insurmountable obstacles—that prevent your characters from reaching their goal. We'll give you some quick and dirty explanations of her method here, but highly encourage you to read her book if you want more information on the subject.

We'll start with a discussion of the character categories.

Role/Pursuit:

This category provides a list of words to help define your character's occupation, story role, or life pursuit. As you can see, we didn't confine ourselves to just one aspect of the word on each card, but tried to provide both positive and negative roles to define heroes or villains as you choose.

Trait:

In this category, we've given you a list of potential character traits that match the word on the card. Again, the traits range from positive to negative since you'll probably want to give your protagonists some flaws along with their positive character traits, and you'll certainly want to do so for your antagonists or villains.

Trait Combined with Role/Pursuit:

Debra Dixon suggests you create a "dominant impression" for each of your characters. This dominant impression uses an adjective and a descriptive noun to define a character, such as a meek waitress, a cocky pilot, or a crusading mortician. It also helps keep your characters clearly in mind as you're writing about them, so you'll have a good idea how they'll react in any given situation.

To create a dominant impression for a new character using this system, draw two cards. Next, look up the first card and select a descriptive noun from the "Role/Pursuit" category, then choose an adjective from the "Trait" category of the other card.

For example, let's say you chose A♣ (Animals) for the trait and 4♦ (Giving) for the role/pursuit. Looking at the options under these cards, you might come up with a kindhearted nurse, a wild missionary, a bestial volunteer, or a xenophobic philanthropist.

So, you needn't be concerned that only fifty-two cards will limit you—these four characters all came from the same two cards, yet they are vastly different.

Goal:

The "G" part of GMC is goal. All major characters have at least one goal, an objective that is vitally important—at least, to them. These goals are those things they want badly enough to take positive action to achieve them. For example, your character might want a better house, a faster car, and a full head of hair, but if he does nothing to go after those goals, they aren't significant to the story or to the reader. But when he spends all of his free time at the gym pumping iron, the reader will conclude that he *is* serious about getting in shape. It then becomes a recognizable goal.

Goals may be internal or external, tangible or intangible, noble or ignoble. In addition, major characters often have more than one goal. Take the movie *Romancing the Stone* for example. Joan Wilder has a couple of different goals that are important to her in the course of the story: she wants to find a dream man like the hero in her novels, and she wants to get a treasure map to Cartagena.

Motivation:

In addition, each goal should have an accompanying motivation. If the goal is *what* the character wants, the motivation is *why* she wants it. For example, Joan's motivation for finding her dream man might be to find love. And her motivation to get the map to Cartagena is very clear—to rescue her sister.

Whatever your character's motivation, it should be strong enough to compel her to take positive action to make her goal happen. And, because one person's goal might be another's motivation, and vice versa, we have combined these two in one category in the card listings.

Conflict:

If the character achieves his goal right away, you don't have a story. So, to make it interesting, you must supply conflict—something keeping him from reaching his goal. Conflict can either be internal (something inside the character) or external (something outside the character).

Using our *Romancing the Stone* example again, Joan's timidity is the internal conflict that keeps her from achieving her goal of finding an adventurous man like her fictional hero. And the villains who try to steal her map are the external conflict keeping her from getting it to her intended destination.

Because internal and external conflicts are entirely different, we've given you a different category for each.

Growth/Realization:

In addition to knowing what your character wants, why he wants it, and what's keeping him from getting it, you also need to know whether or not he achieves it. The answer can be as simple as yes or no . . . or more complex. For example, your hero might achieve his goal but find it isn't what he wanted after all. Or your heroine might fail at achieving hers, but learn something else is really more important to her.

We'll leave it to you to decide whether or not your character achieves his goal, but what is even more important is whether or not he grows or learns anything (comes to realize something important) as a result of your story.

In Joan Wilder's case, she achieves both her goals, and in the process, realizes she's stronger than she ever thought possible.

PLOT CATEGORIES

To discuss plot, we'll use Syd Field's example of story structure. Consider a straight line with five plot points:

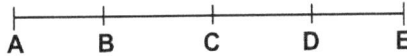

```
├────────┼────────┼────────┼────────┤
A        B        C        D        E
```

This is a rather simple rendition of one possible plot structure, but it makes it easy to discuss. To make it even easier, we've named each point on the line:

A. The Ordinary World
B. The Trigger Event
C. The Change of Plans
D. The Black Moment
E. The Resolution

The Ordinary World:

This term comes from Christopher Vogler's marvelous book, *The Writer's Journey*. Point A, the ordinary world, is often defined in the opening pages of a novel or shortly thereafter, and is the normal milieu for your character (which may not be at all "ordinary" for anyone else), her everyday world before the events of the story take her in a new direction. It helps define the character so that when she is suddenly jerked out of her ordinary world at the next plot point, we understand the significance of the change.

As an example of these five plot points, we'll look at *Star Wars* and the points' effects on the main character, Luke Skywalker. For this particular point, we know that Luke's ordinary world involves working on his uncle's farm on Tattooine at the beginning of the story.

Trigger Event:

The trigger event, point B, is the incident that happens to yank your character out of his secure world and send him in a new direction. It is very close to point A and the beginning of the story because it often happens shortly after the revelation of the ordinary world. In addition, it may help create your character's goal, motivation, and/or conflict for the rest of the story.

That is true in Luke's case when he reaches his trigger event—the murder of his aunt and uncle. Suddenly, nothing will ever be the same again, and he is thrust out of his ordinary world as he joins forces with Obi-wan Kenobi and others to avenge his family and save Princess Leia.

Change of Plans:

To help avoid the dreaded sagging middle syndrome, it is often advisable to have a major event happen at point C—the change of plans.

Once the character is sent in a new direction at B, this change of plans at about the midpoint allows you something to build toward. Then, once the change of plans has been made, it gives your characters something to react to until they hit plot point D. Keep in mind that, in longer stories, you might have several of these turning points.

The change of plans happens for Skywalker when he and his friends are captured by the Death Star. Now, the stakes have risen and Luke must suddenly switch goals to escape his captors and help the rebels.

We combined the trigger event suggestions with the change of plans into one category because they are both essentially changes in the plot. The only difference is where they appear in the story.

Black Moment:

The black moment, point D, is the moment when it appears everything is about to go horribly wrong. The protagonist is about to lose everything she's worked toward, and the villain is about to triumph. This moment appears toward the very end of the book.

For example, in *Star Wars*, several fighters have failed to penetrate the defenses of the Death Star and there are only minutes left to destroy it before it annihilates the rebel base. The black moment occurs just as Luke is about to take his shot when Darth Vader shows up on his tail and locks on to his fighter, spelling doom for our hero.

The Resolution:

Shortly after the black moment, the character makes a decision or has an epiphany that reveals the best course of action. As a result, the character is rewarded (or not, as your plot dictates) and the resolution comes at point E—the end.

In Luke's case, Han Solo distracts Vader long enough for Luke to take fire. Luke decides to trust in the force, so he is able to hit the target, destroy the Death Star, and save the rebel alliance.

We could have made the entries in the character and plot points categories very specific, but we intentionally left them general. This is because, in brainstorming your specific story, it is more useful to say a murder was committed and let you figure out whodunit than to lock you into something too specific such as Colonel Mustard killed Mr. Body in the library with a candlestick.

Now that you have an idea of how the categories are structured, we'll give you some examples of how to build a character or plot from scratch, create an entire story, flesh out an existing character, or find out what happens next in your plot.

2

CREATING A CHARACTER

The process for creating a character is simple. Start by shuffling the deck and selecting seven different cards at random. Choose a role/pursuit for your character from the first card, a trait from the second, and a goal, motivation, internal conflict, external conflict, and growth/realization from subsequent cards.

To give you an idea of the thought process involved, we'll give you a couple of examples. We drew the following cards at random to create a character:

Role/Pursuit: 7♣ (Communication)
Trait: 8♦ (Improvement)
Goal: 9♣ (Deception)
Motivation: K♣ (Ego)
Internal Conflict: J♠ (Rescue)
External Conflict: 8♥ (Time)
Growth/Realization: 8♣ (Death)

Pam decided to write a contemporary romance and create a hero named George. From the list of roles/pursuits under Communication, she chose to make George a publisher.

The next card, Improvement, yields a number of character traits, but Pam decided to make George a progressive publisher who keeps his authors' interests in mind.

What's George's goal? From the list under Deception, she found "Penetrate and reveal a deception." So, she postulated that George knows of a literary agency that uses questionable practices to defraud authors and publishers, and George's goal is to learn exactly what they're doing and reveal it to the world.

Why? What's his motivation? Under Ego, there are a number of choices, but Pam felt none of them fit well with this goal. However, the word "ego" made her think of another possible motivation for George: his ego is at stake because the agency scammed him by convincing him to pay big bucks for a manuscript he later learned was plagiarized. He feels he has to redeem himself and make sure it doesn't happen to anyone else.

Now, what's keeping George from reaching his goal? Under Rescue, Pam found George's internal conflict is "Doubt your ability to save another." George is uncertain of his ability to save others from being defrauded because he has no proof of his allegations—the questionable agency swears they were fooled by the plagiarist as well.

In addition, the Time card gives him an external conflict of "History threatens to repeat itself." It seems the agency has yet another brilliant manuscript he would like to purchase, but rumor has it this story has also been plagiarized.

How does George grow as a result of the story? The Death card gives the following clue: "It's time to stop mourning the past and live in the present." Regardless of how the story comes out, George must give up his fixation on being conned and get on with his life.

So, now Pam has the bare bones of a character, and the seed of a plot. Since this is a romance, she would also need to create a heroine as well, preferably one who is in conflict with the hero. Knowing this, Pam doesn't need to pull a card for the heroine's role/pursuit—it's fairly obvious George's love interest will need to be either the suspected agent or the suspected author. Now that Pam knows that, she can continue using the cards to build the heroine.

Michael used the same cards to create Ellie, the heroine of a mystery. From the Communication card, he chose to give Ellie the role of teacher—a young, footloose substitute teacher.

From the Improvement card, Michael selected a dominant trait of insecurity. It's a trait she badly wants to change—a trait she knows she must change to meet her goal.

Ellie's goal, found under the Deception card, is simple. She wants the truth. She wants to find her sister and discover who she herself is. Ellie remembers her sister from her childhood. Her sister was older than Ellie and took care of her, then disappeared and left her with an old couple who would tell her nothing of her sister, her past, why her sister left, or where she was. But Ellie saw the fear that leaked into their eyes at her insistent questions and they tried to protect her with their silence. However, they are now gone. Their deaths were ruled an accident, but Ellie believes otherwise.

From the list of motivations under Ego, Michael finds "Be successful in your own right." Ellie realizes she cannot attain lasting success without the foundation of belonging somewhere . . . of knowing who she is. She can have no real future without solving her past.

Ellie's internal conflict holds her back. Pulled from the Rescue list, Michael decides that Ellie has a close-held fear that if she frees the truth, she won't survive it.

The Time card provides direction for Ellie's external conflict. Time is her enemy. With each passing day, the trail grows colder, the possibilities fainter. And when the trigger event occurs, time begins to rapidly run out.

From the card of Death, this growth/realization ties it all up: Ellie learns her sister protected her—and paid that price with her life. As did her caretakers. She determines her own life must and will be worthy of those sacrifices. Justice was served. She gets her answers, but they come at an unforeseen price.

3

BUILDING A PLOT

Again, the process is easy. Simply shuffle the cards and draw five cards at random, then select an ordinary world from the first card, a trigger event from the second, a change of plans/turning point from the third, the black moment from the fourth, and a resolution from the fifth.

To give you an example of how it works, we drew the following five cards at random to come up with the bare bones of a plot:

The Ordinary World: J♣ (Desire)
Trigger Event: 6♦ (Heartbreak)
Change of Plans: K♦ (Judgment)
Black Moment: 7♦ (Honor)
Resolution: 4♥ (Sin)

Pam decided to plot a historical novel using these five cards, based in the Victorian period. In reading the five choices for the first card, Desire, Pam was intrigued by the sentence "Having everything you need with no desire for more." She decided to use that for her character's ordinary world—a world in which the heroine, Priscilla, is one of society's darlings, is spoiled rotten, and has everything she'll ever need.

The second card, Heartbreak, yields the following choice for the trigger event that sends the plot in a new direction: "Being dumped." Ah, it seems Priscilla is also engaged to the most sought-after bachelor of the time, but he jilts her at the altar, unable to bear the thought of marrying a spoiled brat.

The third card, Judgment, gives the following choice for the change of plans: "A judgment comes down in your favor." Now the events leading up to the change of plans are clear. Hurt, and with her pride wounded at the thought of being jilted, Priscilla sues her former fiancé for breach of promise. At the midpoint, she wins the lawsuit.

The card drawn for the black moment, Honor, says " You are no longer revered." At this point, Priscilla, who won her lawsuit, nevertheless feels let down by the decision. She has been awarded financial compensation, but it doesn't win her fiancé back. To conceal her mortification, she publicly gloats about her win, coming across as mean-spirited. This causes her actions and her friends' reactions to snowball until she is ostracized from those whose opinions she cares about most.

The last card, Sin, yields the following choice for the resolution: "Forgiving another's sins leads to harmony." At last, the loss of her friends causes Priscilla to understand how petty and spoiled she has been. She forgives her former fiancé for jilting her and apologizes to him and her friends for her behavior. A newly humbled Priscilla regains the love of her friends and family and finds peace and harmony.

Of course, once Pam develops Priscilla's character further and researches the laws and procedures governing breach of promise during this period, the story may change, but this rough sketch of a plot has promise.

Michael used the same cards to plot a modern day action action-adventure tale. Pulled from the Desire card, "On the outside, looking in" grabbed Michael as a great way to set up a story of an ordinary, upper-middle class guy with a safe, boring job. Blane loves action novels and movies. He hungers for adventure and challenge, but his reality is all of ordinary.

The Heartbreak card suggested a couple of nice options to trigger a change for Blane, so Michael decided to use them both. Blane fails to get the big promotion and transfer he's been chasing for six years, and, partially as a result, his wife dumps him.

The wife leaving doesn't surprise and hurt as much as losing out on the promotion. He's known from the beginning that, with her, he was getting great looks coupled with the character depth of spilled paint. This also prepares the reader to accept the next dubious decision Blane will knowingly make—he determines it's time to walk adventure instead of talk it.

The change of plans is provided by the Judgment card. Blane finds himself in serious trouble by exercising poor judgment. He avoids considering all the possible consequences of a little smuggling job when invited by a couple of his new, somewhat shady good-time friends. They were to have the no-brainer anchor leg of the job—the toughest, riskiest parts were to be handled by others. It was supposed to be easy money all wrapped up in a good time.

When the contraband turns out to be a pair of very scared, very blond college girls, Blane knows he's in way over his head. He'd expected guns, computer chips, at worst drugs, but trafficking in white slaves . . . his newly sculpted live-it-up conscience throws a cog.

The "adventure" was innocent enough on paper—a little jungle canoe trip up a couple of snake-infested rivers in Vietnam to deliver the goods to a buyer stuck in some isolated government industrial complex. Now Blane's far from home and facing his black moment. He's in serious trouble. The Honor card suggests this course of action: for Blane to do the honorable thing—refuse to deliver the girls —he will hurt someone he cares very much about. Himself. Not to mention his buddies. If they don't make delivery, they'll anger some very bad people. It's not like he can throw the blondes overboard and run away and hide. Even if he convinces his buddies to do the right thing, the task of getting the girls—and themselves—safely back to the States is seemingly impossible. He has no idea how deep the tentacles of this smuggling operation run. He doesn't know who he can trust.

The Sin card suggests the resolution: Blane knows he must do the right thing, and in doing so, accept the consequences. "Making the right decision brings forgiveness," and for Blane, the right decision is the only acceptable one. He knows he may lose his life trying. Even surviving it, he will be punished for engaging in criminal activities. No matter. It is preferable to life chained to a cursed soul.

4

CREATING AN ENTIRE STORY

To create an entire story from scratch, shuffle the cards and select at least one card for each category. Again, we came up with examples using the following cards:

Role/Pursuit: Q♠ (Revenge)
Trait: J♦ (Insanity)
Goal: Q♣ (Dreams)
Motivation: 10♥ (Unknown)
Internal Conflict: 9♦ (Inheritance)
External Conflict: 5♣ (Burden)
Growth/Realization: K♠ (Riches)
The Ordinary World: 6♣ (Change)
Trigger Event: 6♠ (Magic)
Change of Plans: 4♣ (Build)
Black Moment: A♠ (Knowledge)
Resolution: 7♠ (Misfit)

For this example, Pam chose to write a fantasy. The role/pursuit of the central character of this fantasy is Revenge, and his trait card is

Insanity, which gave Pam a scatterbrained displaced heir she named Skiffy. Obviously, this is *not* a dark fantasy.

Skiffy's goal comes from the Dreams card, showing us that he wants to end someone else's dreams. Specifically, Skiffy is in direct line to the throne, and he wants to end another heir's dreams of seizing it for himself.

What's his motivation? The Unknown card shows that Skiffy wants to make sure he is no longer unknown. He's tired of being hidden and treated like a nobody, so he wants to reveal his noble heritage and take his rightful place.

Unfortunately, his internal conflict, Inheritance, shows that Skiffy fears that claiming his rightful place as heir will also cause him to inherit the family curse. That's why he was hidden—his mother didn't want him to know that he inherited the curse that comes along with the throne.

Scatterbrained Skiffy, however, comes to the conclusion that his mother was overprotective, so he's sure he can avoid whatever she's worried about.

His external conflict, from the Burden card, shows that he feels burdened by others' expectations—his new friends who want to help him claim the throne seem to expect more than he's willing or able to give.

What Skiffy learns at the end comes from the Riches card: "Riches make friends, and adversity proves them." In other words, he learns who his true friends are in adversity.

So, now that we have the outline of Skiffy's character, the plot we put him in is obviously going to be shaped by this character sketch.

Skiffy's ordinary world comes from the Change card—he is unable to escape an unchanging, boring world out in the hinterlands. The trigger event that changes this is from the Magic card: Skiffy suddenly exhibits magical powers that prove he is the missing heir. And his powers are, let's say . . . the ability to call up demons.

Knowing Skiffy's character, we understand that he's so scatterbrained he forgets when and where he left these demons and how to control them, so they have a tendency to cause havoc wherever he goes. Luckily, he only has the power to call up minor imps at this point, but that will change as he gets more powerful. Aha—now we understand the curse as well. This vagueness is also a trait of his ancestors. Since they must continually prove their ability to conjure up demons, they are eventually destroyed by them.

The change of plans at the midpoint comes from the Build card. Skiffy's new friends want to prove he is the rightful heir to the throne, so he is the subject of a huge buildup. It works so well that Skiffy must prove himself by testing his powers against the other claimant. Though he agrees to do so, Skiffy's character sketch shows he isn't so sure he can win this contest . . . or that he even wants to.

The black moment comes in the shape of the Knowledge card. Skiffy's friends have pushed and prodded him into some semblance of readiness by making him into something he's not, and he actually believes he has a chance to win. But at the climax, he realizes that too much knowledge has put him in a dangerous position. If he wins, he'll actually have to be king someday, which will activate the curse and put his life in danger.

The resolution comes from the Misfit card. Skiffy pretends to be more scatterbrained than he really is and throws the contest, refusing to follow in the footsteps of his ancestors by summoning dangerous demons. Breaking the shackles of conformity brings relief, and now that he is no longer heir to the throne, he learns who his real friends are.

Okay, that's Pam's quick and dirty story outline. It's a little rough around the edges and needs some holes filled in, but remember, this is just a first run-through.

Now let's take a look at Michael's foundation for an entire story in the suspense/thriller genre constructed with these same cards. After looking over the possibilities suggested by the role/pursuit category of the Revenge card, Michael decided his main character, Billy Rance, is a vigilante. A really mad, ex-nice guy.

His main character trait, provided by the Insanity card, is that he possesses a brilliant criminal mind without the weakness of conscience to actually be a criminal. And, like many truly brilliant people, he's often in a perpetual fog on matters of practicality, social norms, and common sense.

At this point, Michael is ready to establish the ordinary everyday of Billy's existence. Pulling the Change card and considering the possibilities under the ordinary world heading, Michael likes this: Billy is stuck in stasis. Straitjacketed by a passive, timid approach to life, he drifts with the ebb and flow of life. Even his three-plus years on the job with the FBI hasn't changed that—after all, he's just an analyst.

Even after repeatedly demonstrating his grasp of the criminal mind and his uncanny ability to see possibilities and patterns among a collection of seemingly unconnected facts, he's no more or less than another egghead on the payroll. The glory and the big promotions go to the field agents.

Then he falls for Julie, a rookie field agent just assigned to his district office. He doesn't have the courage to actually tell her how he feels, but she accepts his timid friendship and finds that her academy-basic craft is quickly deepened from their frequent discussions.

What gets this story moving? The Magic card provides the trigger event. Though their friendship had been budding into romance, the magic is lost as treachery snatches her away . . . treachery he saw stalking the agents like a wraith, hunting a victim. He never saw the noose settle around the neck of his beloved.

Billy determines he must act, and his goal is provided by the Dreams card. Billy wants to end the big dreams—the career aspirations—of the FBI field commander, Riz Marvez, who planned, implemented, and led the operation that killed Julie. The whole plan had a fatal flaw, one that he believes Marvez was fully aware of, but deemed an acceptable loss. And it was Julie's life that Marvez spent to buy the successful takedown.

Billy's motivation, from the Unknown card, is simply that he wants to make the unknown known. What the Bureau accepts as a brilliant operation, tainted only by the unfortunate death of an inexperienced agent, Billy wants to expose as a calculated sacrifice of an agent's life to attain an objective—and strip from Marvez the accolades and promotions he reaped for breaking open an incredibly tough, high-profile case.

Billy tries the proper channels but his accusations are rejected outright. His career and job are threatened, so he needs a change of plans. The Build card provides one. Billy must lay the groundwork for a new attack, one that will knock the tainted victory from Marvez's hands. He crafts a complex crime designed to snare Marvez and expose him.

The internal conflict for Billy comes from the Inheritance card. Billy wants justice and to avenge Julie, and he knows how it can be done. But he must face the demon who owns his courage. He has this one chance to marquee this truth: Julie didn't make a stupid mistake —she'd been sacrificed. Will he fumble this chance?

The Burden card provides this external conflict: Billy fears he will collapse under the load. The burden of exposing the Bureau's newly-minted hero adds to the harrowing weight of having failed to act strongly enough on his suspicions the first time.

Billy stands at the jumping-off point. He must act—act or crawl off and choke on his failure. He faces his black moment. The Knowledge card suggests that Billy knows that in order to take down Marvez, he must set into motion his elaborate scheme. But has he forgotten something vital? Will the events dovetail as they must to succeed once Billy turns things loose? Will Marvez be truly forced to choose Billy's solution?

Billy realizes and accepts that while he must stretch himself and take a terrible chance, he isn't reaching beyond his abilities. This resolution comes from the Misfit card—being yourself brings success. The burden of success hangs primarily on the nail of his greatest strength: his genius-like grasp of how to beat the system, to win by breaking the rules and getting away with it.

He pulls on the mask of the vigilante and steps resolutely outside the law. He touches the burning match to the fuse. The game begins. The escapes are narrow, the tensions high, but in the end, Marvez goes down and Billy emerges a better man for his experiences, a more effective man for his ability to actively direct his life.

Pulling the Riches card from the deck here at the growth and realization stage gives Michael the opportunity do something that you will need to do from time to time. Chuck it. Stick it on the bottom. The deck is only a tool, and the options presented by the Riches card don't track with where the story is going. While that could easily become an excuse for not working up a creative sweat, that's not the case here. The strengths and logical progression of the story thus far aren't in the same zip code of the possibilities suggested by the Riches card.

The growth and realization is this: Billy comes to understand and accept that the weight of inaction is a soul-eating burden. That one's life and spirit can be too easily used up in the constant retreat of reaction. Better to act than be acted upon; to be a shaper of possibilities, instead of a victim of circumstance.

As Michael rereads the above paragraph, he realizes that such growth—like all growth—brings with it a payoff . . . .riches of a sort. A better quality of life is of incredible worth, whether brought on by the external forces of wealth or the internal forces of self-improvement and understanding. So, Michael rescues the Riches card from the bottom of the deck. Another lesson offered: the suggested possibilities are not the only possibilities.

5

FLESHING OUT A CHARACTER

If you have a character already developed and just want to learn more about her, you can use the cards to flesh out her bare bones. Merely draw whatever cards you need to expand on her character traits, goals, motivations, etc.

For example, let's take a look at a character we all know—Cinderella. If you're writing a modern version of the rags to riches story and want to know a little bit more about the main character, you might draw a card and read the motivation category to find out why she wants to go to the ball in the first place.

The card we draw is 10 ♠ (Quench), so we read the possible motivations and decide Cindy wants to walk on the wild side for once in her life and indulge her senses. Okay, that gives us a little bit better idea of her character . . . and an entirely different idea of the kind of dance she wants to attend. We could expand on this with additional character traits, conflicts, etc. by drawing additional cards, but you get the idea.

Or, as another example, let's say you've created a character who really intrigues you—an alien stranded on Earth named Xeno. You know his goal is to return home because the Earth's atmosphere is slowly killing him. However, you don't know what his conflict is, so you shuffle and draw two cards to determine his internal and external conflicts.

Xeno's external conflict is shown by the 4♠ (Loyalty) card. A disloyal subordinate, formerly trusted, has betrayed Xeno and his entire clan, leaving him to die on foreign soil. So, Xeno doesn't know who he can trust. And our other card, 9♠ (Pride), shows that his internal conflict is that he's too proud to ask for help so he'll have to find his own way off this miserable planet.

SENDING YOUR PLOT IN A NEW DIRECTION

If you're stuck or blocked and don't know where your recalcitrant characters are taking you next in your plot, you might want to draw a card and read the trigger event/change of plans category.

For example, let's look at Cinderella again and say you want to write a slightly different story, to find out what happens *after* Prince Charming fits the shoe to Cindy's foot. We draw the 6 ♥ (Strength) card and learn that he discovers her Achilles heel. Hmm, you could take this literally or figuratively . . . and we'll leave this decision and plot change as an exercise for the reader.

In Xeno's case, we know his ordinary world is the planet of his origin and that the trigger event is his abandonment on Earth. So, it's obvious that he has to try to survive and find a way to leave, but what's the change of plans in the middle that we're building toward? The 2 ♦ (Family) card suggests that Xeno is shocked when he learns that his family isn't who he thought they were. So who are they? And what role did they play in his abandonment? Finding out the answers will keep us going through to the end of the story.

SOME HINTS ON USING THE CARDS

Since we assume you'll write in a genre you read and are familiar with, we didn't give you a set of choices for selecting one. However, it's important that you do know what genre you want to target *before* you use the cards. As you can see from the preceding examples, the genre helps to shape the characters and plot, and knowing its expectations will help you focus as you draw the cards and create your story.

As you use the cards, keep in mind that their purpose is not to act as a limit on your imagination, but to expand it. So, if a specific card/word doesn't work for you, pull another one. Or, you might brainstorm other associations beyond the definitions provided to learn what it means to you and your story.

Also, it should be obvious that you will use only the cards you need. If you already know your protagonist is a bored housewife, you don't need to know her profession. But you might want to pull a card to read the role/pursuit category and learn what she would *like* to be.

The best way to learn how to use the cards is by doing it, so pick up the deck, shuffle it, and have fun creating your own stories!

PART 2

THE CARDS—CLUBS

A♣ - ANIMALS

CHARACTER

Role/Pursuit: Alien, animal, animal lover, animal trainer, biologist, bitch, blacksmith, breeder, conservationist, cowboy, environmentalist, fisherman, game warden, guide, groomer, hunter, jockey, lion tamer, naturalist, outfitter, rancher, safari leader, shapeshifter, taxidermist, tracker, trapper, trophy hunter, veterinarian, zookeeper

Trait: Amusing, loving, humane, animal lover, tame, devoted, kindhearted, domesticated, exotic, frightened of animals, possessive, primal, wild, bestial, animalistic, xenophobic, savage, feral

Goal/Motivation:
Desire for a pet to love and love you
Protect a beloved animal
Capture or tame a wild creature
Control the animal within
Return to a more basic existence

Internal Conflict:
Animalistic urges threaten everything you hold dear
Love for a pet wars with other needs
Fear or loathing of animals
Overly dependent on animals for love or self-worth
Loss of a pet is devastating

External Conflict:
A dangerous animal threatens your safety
Your pet is threatened/stolen
Lost in the wilderness
A family member demands you give up your pet
You can no longer care for your animals

Growth/Realization:
You must learn to control your baser urges
Every life is precious and animals' lives have value
You are happiest when in tune with nature
If you love something, sometimes you must set it free
You are not alone

PLOT

Ordinary World:
Living surrounded by animals
Caring for animals is the focus of your life
At one with nature
Exploring your baser urges occupies your time
Living peacefully on a farm

Trigger Event/Change of Plans:
A prized animal is threatened
A domesticated animal reverts to the wild state
Challenged to contend in a sporting competition

Finding an abandoned/injured animal
A wild animal attacks

Black Moment:
An animal's life hangs in the balance
Cornered by a wild animal with nowhere to go
Must choose between a pet's safety and your own
An animal offers to sacrifice its life for yours
Giving in to animalistic urges is tempting

Resolution:
Caging the wild beast brings safety
The love of an animal helps you succeed
Controlling your baser urges leads to success
Returning to nature makes you happy
Saving an animal helps you save yourself

2♣ – APPRENTICESHIP

CHARACTER

Role/Pursuit: Apprentice, child, clerk, entry-level position, gopher, greenhorn, heir, helper, hireling, intern, newcomer, novice, peon, protégé, pup, recruit, rookie, slave, student, tenderfoot, understudy, wannabe

Trait: Studious, ambitious, enthusiastic, childlike, diligent, thirsty for knowledge, unseasoned, inexperienced, driven, uneducated, unskilled, naive, clumsy, ignorant, clueless, downtrodden, insecure, callow, tyrannized

Goal/Motivation:
Learn more about the situation, another character, or life itself
Achieve a higher level/promotion
Enter a higher social class or level of existence
Improve current skills or master a new one
Win a competition proving mastery of your profession

Internal Conflict:
Lack the necessary skills
Doubting your ability to succeed
Fear of success
Fear of failure
Fearing it will take too long to master the necessary skills

External Conflict:
Social/Job position is too low or holds you back
Can't hold a job
Can't obtain necessary training or the goal is too difficult
Others cast doubt on your skills
Others are more skilled or have achieved a higher level

Growth/Realization:
You still have a lot to learn
Others have much to teach you
The position you thought you wanted isn't what you wanted after all
You don't have what it takes to succeed
You learned a lot despite the odds

PLOT

Ordinary World:
Attending a school or other academic environment
Working in the lower rungs of a company/social structure
Growing up in a safe, comfortable learning environment
Living subject to a master
Waiting for the opportunity to move into a higher situation

Trigger Event/Change of Plans:
Receive an offer of employment beyond your current capability
The chance to start over in a new profession, perhaps something more creative

Suddenly moved into a position you're not qualified for
A superior dies or vanishes and you must take over
Suddenly thrust into a situation where you must master new skills

Black Moment:

You lack the mastery to complete the goal
You're fired or remove from your position, or working in your chosen
profession is no longer possible
You learned more than you ever wanted to know or your knowledge
is dangerous
Now that you have achieved mastery of your goal, life is boring and
meaningless
You don't have what it takes

Resolution:

New acquired skills give you the capability to succeed
Achieve a higher level/promotion
Enter a higher social class or level of existence
Prove mastery of your profession
Start over to learn a new profession

3♣ – BALANCE

CHARACTER

Role/Pursuit: Accountant, arbiter, chemist, commentator, counselor, environmentalist, gymnast, ironworker, journalist, judge, juggler, law enforcer, magistrate, mediator, negotiator, philosopher, porter, referee, spiritualist, suffragette, tightrope walker

Trait: Fair, harmonious, balanced, congenial, calm, sedate, poised, moderate, harmonious, zen-like, sane, just, prudent, levelheaded, temperate, steady, unchanging, manic-depressive, unbalanced, unfair, moody

Goal/Motivation:
Achieve balance in your life
Unbalance the status quo
Make ends meet
Find harmony
Tip the balance in your favor

Internal Conflict:
Lack of balance in your life
Can't maintain emotional equilibrium
Living in an inharmonious atmosphere
Feeling on the edge of insanity
Inability to decide between two equal choices

External Conflict:
Stuck between a rock and a hard place
Being the victim of injustice
Having to deal with unbalanced people
The status quo is threatened by drastic change
Too many balls in the air at once

Growth/Realization:
Can't remain in stasis forever
Can no longer sit on the fence—must commit to something
Happiness lies in balance and moderation
Life is unfair
Perfect balance and harmony isn't all it's cracked up to be

PLOT

Ordinary World:
Balancing more than one job to make ends meet
Living in a constant state of indecision
Life is in perfect balance
Plagued by misfortune
Dedicated to achieving harmony and balance in all things

Trigger Event/Change of Plans:
Thrown off-balance by an unexpected event
The status quo is disrupted
The balance of power is shifted

An unfair act puts your life's balance in jeopardy
Harmony is shattered by an unforeseen event

Black Moment:
Life hangs in the balance
Action will irrevocably shift the balance of power
Teetering on the edge of disaster
Poised between two equally bad choices
You drop the ball

Resolution:
Restoring balance and harmony brings fulfillment
Taking action shifts the balance of power
The old balance is changed forever, bringing a new balance
Tipping the balance in someone else's favor brings you success
Life will never be in balance again . . . and that's okay

4♣ – BUILD

CHARACTER

Role/Pursuit: Agent, architect, assassin, boatwright, bodybuilder, builder, composer, construction worker, cooper, craftsman, creator, demolition expert, designer, destroyer, developer, draftsman, engineer, founder, invader, inventor, mad scientist, maker, manufacturer, map maker, pioneer, planner, producer, raider, wrecker

Trait: Ambitious, enterprising, visionary, ground breaker, idealistic, shaper, prescient, innovative, pioneering, opportunistic, destructive, scheming, calculating, malicious, damaging

Goal/Motivation:
Build for the future and/or a better life
Build a monument to someone or something
Stop the construction of something
Build something no one has seen before
Build a better mousetrap

Internal Conflict:

A tendency to build castles in the air
Can't stop destructive behavior
You have built your expectations too high
Your plans are built on false assumptions
Fearing you have built a monster

External Conflict:

Someone is trying to destroy what you have built
Someone claims your workmanship is shoddy
Another's construction is damaging or destructive
You are forbidden to build further
Your construction is dangerous

Growth/Realization:

Rome was not built in a day
Never tear a building down from the bottom up
If you build a better mousetrap, the world will beat a path to
your door
Building is more satisfying than destroying
What was built once can be built again

PLOT

Ordinary World:

Building for the future
In the construction industry
Trying to rebuild your life
Building yourself up
Trying to stop construction of something harmful

Trigger Event/Change of Plans:

You are the subject of a huge buildup
New construction threatens your livelihood

You lay the groundwork for something new
Sudden destruction changes your life
New construction is completed

Black Moment:

Imminent destruction of all you have built
Your plans come to naught
Continuing to build on your success harms others
You are doomed by what others have built
What you have engineered comes tumbling down

Resolution:

You reap what you have sowed
You built well, bringing success
You rise from your own ashes to build anew
Building others up gives you satisfaction
The right choice helps you build a better future

5♣ – BURDEN

CHARACTER

Role/Pursuit: Beast of burden, carrier, CEO, clan head, commanding officer, construction worker, drudge, factory worker, failure, farmer, flunky, laborer, martyr, menial, mover, porter, servant, sinner, slave, sweatshop worker, trucker

Trait: Responsible, strong, dutiful, caring, powerful, reliable, hard-working, overloaded, long-suffering, struggling, oppressed, handi-capped, ignorant, poverty-stricken, weighed down with responsibilities, overburdened, weak, irresponsible

Goal/Motivation:
Get rid of a burden
Lighten the load for yourself or another
Gain the strength to carry a burden
Share or transfer your burden
Avoid responsibility

Internal Conflict:
The weight of the world is on your shoulders
Burdened with guilt
Feeling too weak to cope
Unable to say "no"
Duty and responsibility war with hoped-for freedom

External Conflict:
Burdened by needy others
Carrying too many responsibilities
Burdened by others' expectations of you
Oppressed by unwanted circumstances
Crumbling under the load

Growth/Realization:
Sharing the burden lightens the load
Sometimes you have to say "no"
A voluntary burden is no burden
Life goes on, despite the heavy load
Shedding unwanted responsibilities doesn't make you a bad person

PLOT

Ordinary World:
Laden with many responsibilities
Struggling to carry the burden alone
Free of responsibilities and burdens
Unable to face life and all its burdens
Avoiding responsibility

Trigger Event/Change of Plans:
Gaining yet another unwanted burden
Suddenly thrust into a position of grave responsibility
Your onerous responsibilities suddenly disappear

Someone offers to share the load
You get saddled with responsibilities—again

Black Moment:

One more burden threatens to break you
You are tempted to bow out of all your responsibilities
You ignore your responsibilities once too often
Undecided whether to take on someone else's heavy burden
Your responsibilities are too overwhelming to survive

Resolution:

The burden is lifted, bringing relief
You take responsibility for your own actions
Taking responsibility for others gives satisfaction
Sharing the burden lightens the load
Others become stronger because you let them carry their own burden

6♣ – CHANGE

CHARACTER

Role/Pursuit: Actor, adventurer, cashier, catalyst, gambler, historian, invader, inventor, merchant, meteorologist, reformer, researcher, revolutionary, social worker, sociologist, stand-in, substitute, trader, union leader, usurper

Trait: Daring, adventurous, idealistic, forward-thinking, whimsical, mercurial, evolved, chameleon, comfortable, changeable, fickle, thrill-seeker, variable, erratic, inflexible, easily bored, moody, temperamental

Goal/Motivation:
Change your life radically
Maintain the status quo at all costs
Seek out all the thrills life has to offer
Minimize the changes in your life
Make yourself over into someone/something different

Internal Conflict:
Fear of change
Unwilling to change
Too erratic to commit to anything
Unable to cope with rapid changes
Bored with lack of change

External Conflict:
Life changes too rapidly
Forced into an unchanging, boring existence
Another's internal changes disrupt your life
Forced to change despite your protests
Life is too changeable and unsettling

Growth/Realization:
To change the world, you must first change yourself
We do not always gain by changing
Variety is the spice of life
Nothing is permanent but change
The more things change, the more they remain the same

PLOT

Ordinary World:
Living on the edge and seeking thrills
Constantly on the move, changing from place to place
Living the same life your parents did
Unable to escape an unchanging world
In stasis

Trigger Event/Change of Plans:
Changing lives with someone else
Thrust into sudden and rapid change of circumstances
Altering your appearance radically

Another tries to change you
You attempt to change someone else

Black Moment:

You are forced to change or suffer the consequences
Changing your mind will hurt someone else
Another's unexpected change affects you dramatically
The right decision will change your life forever
A shocking change is the only answer

Resolution:

Changing your mind/plan results in a win-win situation
Persuading others to change achieves your goal
Adapting to change brings you a happier life
Refusing to change makes life less challenging
Accepting the lack of change brings peace

7♣ – COMMUNICATION

CHARACTER

Role/Pursuit: Agent, announcer, artist, comedian, communicator, delivery boy, entertainer, gossip, herald, informant, interpreter, journalist, liaison, librarian, lisper, messenger, mime, negotiator, operator, preacher, public relations, publisher, speaker, stutterer, tattletale, teacher, terrorist

Trait: Perceptive, talkative, intuitive, demonstrative, candid, enthusiastic, charismatic, open, outgoing, tactful, friendly, uses malaprops, gabby, terse, tactless, outspoken, blunt, sarcastic, indiscreet, nosy, nag, blowhard, libelous, slanderous

Goal/Motivation:
Communicate more effectively
Stop the spread of harmful gossip
Spread the word about something that excites you
Get the whole story
Tell your story to the world

Internal Conflict:

Unable to communicate effectively

Unable to express emotions

Withholding information is hurting others

Telling the truth is painful

Your nonverbal signals don't match your verbal ones

External Conflict:

Gossip or lies are hurting you or your loved ones

Unable to get your message across to another

Held incommunicado

Lies are coming back to haunt you

Others are urging you to tell the truth

Growth/Realization:

You don't have to tell everything you know

Confession is good for the soul

Liars never prosper

Sometimes they shoot the messenger

It is better to be thought a fool than to open your mouth and prove it

PLOT

Ordinary World:

Living in a small town rife with gossip

Entertaining others with made-up stories

Being the nexus of a communication network

Living in a society that has no free speech

Guarding dangerous information with your life

Trigger Event/Change of Plans:

You decide to get it off your chest and tell the world

You lose freedom of speech

A harmful lie is spread about you or your loved ones

Dangerous information has gotten loose
A strange message arrives, bringing disquieting news

Black Moment:
You are threatened with having your secret exposed
Breaking the story will harm an innocent
The message goes astray, undoing your plans
You discover dangerous information that threatens your life
Keeping quiet is no longer an option

Resolution:
Telling the truth results in a win-win situation
Speaking your mind brings relief
Keeping your mouth shut is best for all concerned
Confession brings absolution
Suppressing a story is more honorable than telling it

8♣ – DEATH

CHARACTER

Role/Pursuit: Animator, assassin, doctor, drug dealer, firefighter, ghost, grave robber, healer, last of a dying breed, monster, mortician, murderer, necromancer, nurse, organ/blood donor, paramedic, police officer, sniper, soldier, survivor, undertaker, vampire, zombie

Trait: Peaceful, passive, aloof, unworried, detached, neutral, withdrawn, indifferent, atrophied, stagnant, worried, fear of death, unhealthy, morbid, victimized, murderous, suicidal, dying, corrupt, dead, extinct

Goal/Motivation:
Start all over again
Recover from the death of a loved one
Remove someone from this plane of existence
Learn the truth about a loved one's death
Cheat death

Internal Conflict:
Your skills are obsolete
You are dying inside
Fear of death
A phobia makes you deathly afraid
You are dead to all hope

External Conflict:
A homicidal maniac is on the loose
A life-threatening situation erupts
A loved one's life is in danger
You are forced to kill or be killed
The death of another is devastating

Growth/Realization:
Life goes on
Nothing is certain but death and taxes
Death is the only permanent solution
Life is precious—live every moment as if it were your last
It's time to stop mourning the past and live in the present

PLOT

Ordinary World:
Living on the edge
Surrounded by death and/or destruction
The line between life, death, and afterlife is blurred
In constant expectation of death
Living life to its fullest

Trigger Event/Change of Plans:
The death of your hopes and dreams
A sudden death rocks your world
Experiencing a near-death event

Your period of mourning is complete
The rebirth of something you never thought possible

Black Moment:
Your life hangs by a thread
Another's life is threatened
Your hopes and dreams are about to die
You want to give up the ghost
Total destruction is imminent

Resolution:
The death of your adversary brings closure
The death of one dream begets another
Cheating death gives you a new appreciation for life
Learning there is life after death brings relief
The time for mourning is over—it's time to get on with your life

9♣ – DECEPTION

CHARACTER

Role/Pursuit: Actor, bigamist, carny, cheater, con artist, decoy, gold digger, grifter, hypochondriac, illusionist, impostor, intelligence agent, liar, magician, masked hero, model, photographer, plastic surgeon, politician, prankster, propagandist, shapeshifter, spy, thief, trickster, twin, writer

Trait: Truthful, clever, cunning, adroit, nimble, wily, adept, persuasive, risk-taker, inscrutable, deceptive, disguised, fearful, prideful, secretive, sly, self-deceiving, hypocritical, insincere, contradictory, dishonest, malicious

Goal/Motivation:
Deceive others
Penetrate and reveal a deception
Learn the truth
Stop fooling yourself
Spin doctor an event to make it more palatable

Internal Conflict:

Hating the necessity for deceiving others
Refusing to lie, no matter what the consequences
Unable to discern who's telling the truth
Lying to yourself
Enjoying the practice of deception

External Conflict:

A loved one is being conned
Someone is deceiving you "for your own good"
Someone is trying to penetrate your deception
You are forced to deceive others against your will
Someone else's deception threatens you

Growth/Realization:

Honesty is the best policy
Small deceptions smooth life's rough edges
You've been fooling yourself all along
Fool me once, shame on you; fool me twice, shame on me
Deception sometimes serves a higher purpose

PLOT

Ordinary World:

Caught up in a web of deception and lies
Living in disguise or in hiding
Fooling yourself about your talents and success
Living a lie
Being scrupulously honest

Trigger Event/Change of Plans:

Defrauded by a trickster
Learning everything you believed in is built on lies
Learning the entire world is being deceived

Telling one lie snowballs into many others
Deciding to deceive someone

Black Moment:

The fragile structure built on lies is about to topple
Learning everything is based on lies
Revealing a deception will harm another
Your deception is revealed
Realizing you've been fooling yourself

Resolution:

Telling the truth brings relief despite the consequences
Maintaining a deception is best for all concerned
Revealing another's deception brings deserved retribution
Exposing a charlatan to a select few saves face
Stop fooling yourself so you can get on with your life

10♣ – DEPENDENCE

CHARACTER

Role/Pursuit: Acolyte, aide, ally, armsman, assistant, child, dependent, deputy, domestic, employee, farmer, henchman, liegeman, minor, mistress, panhandler, servant, spouse, stooge, subordinate, toady, underling, vassal, ward, welfare recipient

Trait: Supportive, trusting, faithful, adoring, helpful, modest, vulnerable, childlike, domestic, meek, unpretentious, clinging, henpecked, fawning, resentful, impotent, powerless, weak, spineless, downtrodden, enslaved

Goal/Motivation:
Become independent
Get rid of hangers-on
Find someone to lean on
Break the bonds of co-dependence
Regain control of your life

Internal Conflict:
Too independent to accept help
Overly dependent on others
Don't know how to form an opinion of your own
Hate being unable to control your own destiny
Have only yourself to depend on

External Conflict:
Too many needy people depend on you
Others try to control you
Others accuse you of being too dependent
Others try to sever your comfortable dependent relationship
Your independence is threatened

Growth/Realization:
The only one you can depend on is yourself
Being independent is worth the cost
You don't have to feel needed to be loved
Sometimes you have to lean on someone else
It all depends on whose ox is gored

PLOT

Ordinary World:
Struggling to assert yourself or your work
Have no one to depend on but yourself
Being overly dependent on someone else
Having too many needy people depending on you
Being independent

Trigger Event/Change of Plans:
Your only means of support is removed
Free at last of clinging dependents
Thrust into depending on another

Losing your independence
Gaining independence at last

Black Moment:

Your independence is threatened
Realizing you can't depend on anyone else to save you
Winning comes with too many strings attached
Losing someone you depended on is devastating
The ties of dependence are overwhelming

Resolution:

To survive, you must cut the ties of dependence
Giving up a little independence leads to success
Allowing yourself to depend on others is a relief
Letting others depend on you is satisfying
Achieving independence and freedom is all that matters

J♣ – DESIRE

CHARACTER

Role/Pursuit: Addict, applicant, aspirant, candidate, concubine, courtesan, dictator, fugitive, gambler, gigolo, heir, hunter, junkie, leader, lecher, performer, prisoner, researcher, scholar, seeker, slave, social climber, understudy, usurper, virgin

Trait: Agreeable, charming, popular, innocent, wistful, focused, hungry, thirsty, ambitious, single-minded, driven, needy, passionate, sensuous, puritan, covetous, lovesick, obsessive, impatient, desperate, lustful, impoverished, wanton, lascivious

Goal/Motivation:
Find what is missing in your life
Desperately wanting a situation to change
Establish a deeper bond
Desire for something unattainable
Find fulfillment

Internal Conflict:
Your desire consumes you to the exclusion of all else
What you desire most is forbidden
Your desire conflicts with common sense
Fearing you want too much
You desire nothing

External Conflict:
You are addicted to something or someone
What you want most in life is unattainable
Someone is keeping you from what you desire most
Another's desire is disrupting your life
Expressing your desire hurts someone else

Growth/Realization:
Be careful what you wish for
Getting what you need is better than getting what you want
Anticipation is more satisfying than consummation
Sometimes it's necessary to put your desires on hold
The end is not worth the means

PLOT

Ordinary World:
Wanting something so badly any means is acceptable
Consumed solely with thoughts of the goal
Being addicted to something or someone
Having everything you need with no desire for more
On the outside, looking in

Trigger Event/Change of Plans:
An encounter with sexual undertones disturbs or excites you
An unattainable desire suddenly seems possible
Offered the fulfillment of every desire—with a catch

Suddenly obsessed with a desire for something or someone
Learning of another's obsession

Black Moment:
Your desires threaten to overwhelm you
Your addiction or hidden desires are exposed
Loss of what you desire most in life
Achieving your goal is no longer satisfying
Another's desire threatens you

Resolution:
Understanding your greatest desire can never be realized
Achieving your goal brings contentment
A hidden desire is fulfilled before the need is expressed
You learn to settle for less because you set your sights too high
Postponing gratification brings harmony

Q♣ – DREAMS

CHARACTER

Role/Pursuit: Athlete, astronaut, celebrity, competitor, dreamer, fairy, fashion designer, idealist, illusionist, inventor, medium, monster, performer, phantasm, philanthropist, philosopher, pioneer, poet, scientist, sleepwalker, understudy, visionary, youth

Trait: Adventurous, imaginative, creative, whimsical, romantic, dreamy, starry-eyed, prescient, idealistic, pensive, abstracted, foolish, vague, scatterbrained, impractical, shiftless, unrealistic, delusional

Goal/Motivation:
Achieve a dream
Rid yourself of recurring nightmares
Create a utopia
End someone else's dreams
Learn to live in the real world

Internal Conflict:
Your dreams are impractical
Dreaming is more fun than coping with reality
Fearing your dreams are unattainable
You are afraid to dream
Having unfulfilled dreams hurts too much

External Conflict:
Your fantasy bubble is punctured
Someone wants to take away your dream
Your dreams become the object of public ridicule
Someone else's dreams threaten yours
Dreaming is prohibited

Growth/Realization:
You must follow your dreams
Dreaming is for fools
Closing a door opens a window
If you dream, dream big
If you leap, the net will appear

PLOT

Ordinary World:
Lost in a dream world
Plagued by nightmares
Going all out for your dreams
Living without dreams
Living in utopia

Trigger Event/Change of Plans:
Daydreaming gets you in trouble
A dream portends disaster
Your nightmares come to life

Your dream becomes reality
Your dreams are threatened

Black Moment:

Your dreams are shattered
The right decision will make you lose your dreams forever
Dreams come back to haunt you
Fulfillment of your dreams bring disaster
You must ignore your own dreams to save another

Resolution:

Doing what you love will make the money follow
You can have your cake and eat it, too
You learn to live in the real world
Fulfilling your dreams brings contentment
Helping someone else achieve their dream brings satisfaction

K♣ – EGO

CHARACTER

Role/Pursuit: Artist, celebrity, commander, counselor, dictator, egotist, hypnotist, hypochondriac, leader, mentor, mogul, philanthropist, politician, professor, psychiatrist, psychologist, saint, scholar, scientist, therapist

Trait: Selfless, dedicated, helpful, generous, receptive, proud, oblivious, flamboyant, penetrating, dramatic, insecure, close-minded, self-satisfied, smug, egotistical, didactic, jealous, braggart, arrogant, spiteful, big-headed

Goal/Motivation:
Be successful in your own right
Be at the top of your profession
Learn what makes another tick
Learn what you're good at
Control your own ego

Internal Conflict:
Afraid you're not good enough/not knowing your own worth
Feeling you're too good for this
Hiding the true nature of your talent or intelligence
Feeling a loss of control over your mental faculties
Afraid you'll appear conceited

External Conflict:
Others try to bring you down a peg
Others try to destroy your ego
Others try to make you think you're crazy
Circumstances make you feel inept
Your identity is threatened

Growth/Realization:
You have much to learn
Vanity led you to overestimate your abilities
You are better than you ever thought possible
You were wrong
The way to a man's heart is through his ego

PLOT

Ordinary World:
Confident that you are the best you can be
Helping others deal with their insecurities
You are the center of the known universe
At the bottom of the food chain
Cowed by someone else's ego

Trigger Event/Change of Plans:
Suddenly losing all confidence
A challenge to your ego arises
Unexpected success makes you feel you can take on the world

Your identity is stolen
Another's overwhelming ego affects you adversely

Black Moment:
You fear losing your hold on reality
Doing the right thing will be a devastating blow to your ego
Your insecurities make you unable to choose
Action will reveal your security to be a sham
Your very identity is threatened

Resolution:
Revealing your insecurities is the only way to grow
Putting your ego on hold for another's benefit brings satisfaction
Renewed confidence in your own abilities gives you the ability to win
You don't have to be number one to win
You don't need to hide your light under a bushel to be loved

PART 3

THE CARDS—DIAMONDS

A ◆ – FAITH

CHARACTER

Role/Pursuit: Acolyte, agnostic, angel, apostle, atheist, bard, believer, bishop, choir member, churchgoer, cleric, deity, devil, disciple, faith healer, medium, minister, monk, nun, priest, rabbi, saint, shaman, witch, witch doctor, zealot

Trait: Faithful, serene, devout, forgiving, trusting, true, loyal, pious, saintly, supportive, charitable, patriotic, righteous, unerring, resolute, enduring, devilish, skeptical, faithless, impious, dishonest, traitorous, satanic

Goal/Motivation:
Regain faith in yourself
Convert others to your faith
Find faith in something or someone
Show others you can be trusted
Prove someone is unfaithful

Internal Conflict:
Possessing no faith in yourself
Unable to trust others
Having no faith in anything
Fearing your faith is misplaced
Tempted to be unfaithful

External Conflict:
No one trusts you
A loved one is unfaithful
A friend betrays your trust
The foundations of your faith are tested
Your faith is challenged or attacked

Growth/Realization:
A faithful friend is better than gold
The only one you can trust is yourself
Faith can move mountains
Being trusted is a better compliment than being loved
Having faith doesn't mean you shouldn't keep rowing for shore

PLOT

Ordinary World:
Trusting in the Lord to provide
Surrounded by the faithful
Living in a faithless world
Having complete faith in someone or something
Your faith is continuously challenged

Trigger Event/Change of Plans:
Your faith is tested
Losing faith in someone
Learning your faith is misplaced

A loved one is unfaithful
Learning your faith has been based on a lie

Black Moment:
Faced with a complete loss of faith
Afraid trusting someone will bring failure
You can't trust yourself to do the right thing
Your faith in another is shattered
Being unfaithful appears the only choice

Resolution:
To win, you must let go and have faith
Trusting in someone brings success
Trusting in yourself helps you succeed
Having faith brings reward
Remaining true to your faith brings happiness

2◆ – FAMILY

CHARACTER

Role/Pursuit: Adopted, archeologist, aristocrat, blended family member, brat, child care provider, foster parent, foundling, gang member, genealogist, homemaker, housekeeper, illegitimate child, mobster, matriarch, mistress, patriarch, parent, sociologist, spouse

Trait: Home-loving, fostering, caring, nurturing, loving, loyal, noble, unselfish, pregnant, family-oriented, comfort-loving, childless, homeless, divorced, nepotistic, disinherited, insular, isolated, incestuous, adulterous, disloyal

Goal/Motivation:
Reconcile with an estranged family member
Have a family of your own
Escape from an oppressive family
Learn who your family is
Help your family

Internal Conflict:
Disliking a family member
Family loyalty wars with other needs
Not knowing who your family is
Lack of family ties
Inability to care about family

External Conflict:
Oppressed or stifled by a family member
Overburdened by a demanding family
Considered the black sheep of the family
Disinherited by your family or cut off
Plagued by infertility

Growth/Realization:
Family members make the best friends
Blood is thicker than water
There's no place like home
You can't go home again
Family ties are the only lasting ones

PLOT

Ordinary World:
Living in the bosom of a large family
Homeless
Oppressed by family expectations
Estranged from your family
Looking for a family to belong to

Trigger Event/Change of Plans:
You are suddenly homeless
You learn of a skeleton in the family closet
Your family is threatened

Learning your family isn't who you thought they were
Suddenly cut off from your family

Black Moment:

Action will ruin your family
Doing the right thing will cost you your family
You become hopelessly mired in family obligations
You are about to lose all chances for a happy family life
You are about to be cut off from family forever

Resolution:

Your family rallies around to help you succeed
Doing the right thing brings family support
Helping a family member brings success
Though you lose a friend, you gain a family
You learn who your true family and friends are

3◆ – FEAR

CHARACTER

Role/Pursuit: Assassin, boss, blackmailer, bully, captive, criminal, daredevil, despot, dictator, enforcer, extortionist, gang member, hero, hunter, inquisitor, invader, killer, law enforcer, mobster, monster, prey, psychopath, sadist, secret police, soldier, terrorist, thrill-seeker, tyrant, victim, villain

Trait: Brave, heroic, bold, intrepid, fearless, courageous, reckless, cautious, worrywart, shy, foolish, apprehensive, autocratic, intimidating, paranoid, victimized, fearful, cowardly, ruthless, heartless, cold-blooded, monstrous, lawless, immoral

Goal/Motivation:
Master your fear
Eliminate the source of your fear
Escape from fear

Overcome a phobia
Instill fear in others

Internal Conflict:
Overwhelmed by fear
Fear of making the wrong choice
Fear of failure or success
A phobia makes you afraid
Fear of losing someone or something

External Conflict:
A catastrophe is imminent
Forced to face your fears
You're trapped
Your life is threatened
Someone else's fears are affecting your life

Growth/Realization:
You cannot let fear control your life
Fear has made you stronger
What you feared is not so bad after all
You must press on, despite your fear
The reward is worth the risk

PLOT

Ordinary World:
Fearing a negative situation will come to pass
Living life on the edge
Living in an oppressed situation
Being too timid to take risks
Life is happy and free of fear

Trigger Event/Change of Plans:

A negative confrontation puts fear in your heart
Tired of being afraid, you act
A death threat arrives
Disaster strikes
You're required to do what you fear most

Black Moment:
You come face to face with what you fear most
You fear achieving your goal will not be as good as you hope
The price of failure is too high
You're paralyzed with fear and unable to act
You've taken too many risks and this one threatens to ruin all

Resolution:
Facing your fears enables you to come out ahead
You conquer what you feared most
Taking risks makes life richer
You are no longer afraid of what you once feared
Fear no longer has the power to control your actions

4◆ – GIVING

CHARACTER

Role/Pursuit: Backer, banker, channeler, charity worker, cheapskate, fairy godmother, hoarder, mentor, miser, missionary, nun, nurse, parent, patron, philanthropist, physician, scrooge, sponsor, teacher, venture capitalist, volunteer

Trait: Generous, liberal, charitable, warm, loving, kind, considerate, giving, supportive, nurturing, thoughtful, conscientious, big-hearted, acquisitive, possessive, grasping, monopolizing, greedy, selfish, materialistic, tightfisted, voracious, stingy, self-absorbed, cheap

Goal/Motivation:
Feel needed
Help others
Learn to be more giving
Teach others to be more giving
Learn to share

Internal Conflict:

You give too much
Unable to give to anyone else
Accepting charity is abhorrent
Afraid you'll give away too much
You don't have anything to give

External Conflict:

You can't give enough to satisfy everyone
A loved one is too possessive
Another's gifts make you feel obligated
You are accused of not being able to give
Someone threatens to give you away

Growth/Realization:

It is better to give than to receive
It is not only what we give, but how we give that counts
You can't give what you haven't got
Give and you shall receive
Don't look a gift horse in the mouth

PLOT

Ordinary World:

Living on charity
Selfless and dedicated to charity works
Selfish and concerned only about yourself
In a possessive relationship
In a giving and loving relationship

Trigger Event/Change of Plans:

You receive an unexpected gift
Someone gives you away
Someone's generosity changes your life

You decide to give away something precious
You are forced to accept charity

Black Moment:
Your selfishness brings you to the point of ruin
Your generosity is revealed as a sham
You are tapped out with nothing left to give
Your well-meaning generosity is thrown back in your face
Someone is about to take everything you hold dear

Resolution:
Give your adversary enough rope and he'll hang himself
Giving and loving make life worth living
Giving of yourself brings happiness
Another's selfishness is exposed
Being generous to others bestows success upon you

5 ◆ – HEALTH

CHARACTER

Role/Pursuit: ambulance chaser, caregiver, chiropractor, dentist, dietician, doctor, EMT, gerontologist, healer, hypochondriac, lab technician, labor coach, malingerer, medic, naturopath, nurse, optometrist, organ donor, organ stealer, patient, personal injury lawyer, pharmacist, poisoner, psychiatrist, quack, radiologist, serial killer, shaman, snake oil salesman, surgeon, therapist

Trait: healthy, fit, vigorous, virile, strong, athletic, hearty, nurturing, healing, protective, supportive, caring, helpful, fertile, feeble, weak, obese, obsessive-compulsive, bedridden, physically handicapped, blind, deaf, disease-ridden, terminally ill, mentally unstable, suicidal, murderous

Goal/Motivation:
Heal or escape from your affliction/regain the health you once lost
Find a cure for another's affliction
Protect someone who cannot protect themselves

Learn what is causing an illness or affliction
Gain the physical and mental strength to do what is needed

Internal Conflict:

Ill health keeps you from pursuing your goal
Fear you will make someone ill
The person who needs your help doesn't deserve it
Achieving health will jeopardize your goal
Fear you don't know enough to help yourself or a patient

External Conflict:

Someone is trying to harm you physically or mentally
A deadly disease is on the loose
You are prevented from helping someone
Someone else's ill health prevents you from achieving your objective
A medical professional forbids you from performing an action

Growth/Realization:

The cure you needed was there all along or you were never ill to
begin with
Good health is a prerequisite for happiness
Nothing is worth endangering your health or others'
Risking your health is a small price to pay for success
You do not have to be perfectly healthy to succeed

PLOT

Ordinary World:

Working as a healer and helping those around you
Searching for a cure
Helping those who have had their health compromised by others
Acting as a caregiver for an ailing family member
Living with a chronic disease or condition

Trigger Event/Change of Plans:

A sudden illness changes everything

You discover someone's health or life is being targeted

You learn of a miracle cure

A deadly disease has been released

You must suddenly become a caregiver

Black Moment:

The patient is about to die

The cure is a failure

Your illness jeopardizes your success

The villain is not as ill as you hoped

The cure is worse than the disease

Resolution:

A cure is found/the patient recovers

Embracing your condition brings relief

Helping others brings satisfaction

Saving someone else helps you save yourself

Healthy practices help you achieve miracles

6♦ – HEARTBREAK

CHARACTER

Role/Pursuit: Adulterer, cardiologist, casualty, con artist, counselor, entertainer, healer, heartbreaker, jilt, kidnapper, lover, mistress, playboy, prostitute, psychiatrist, savior, survivor, thief, vamp, victim, widow(er)

Trait: Comforting, joyous, soothing, happy, invigorating, content, heartbroken, humorous, relieved, grateful, enduring, apprehensive, grieving, despondent, jilted, suffering, anguished, heartsick, heartless, uncaring, unfeeling, cold, selfish, callous

Goal/Motivation:
Recover from loss of another
Win back significant other
Get rid of admirer
Refrain from hurting someone else
Never be hurt again

Internal Conflict:

Fear of losing love

Heartbreak makes you unable to cope

Life seems meaningless because of the pain

Afraid no one will love you again

Fear of being hurt

External Conflict:

Dumped by a lover

There is a rival for your loved one's affection

The loss of something or someone important

Someone is trying to take love away from you

A loved one is heartbroken

Growth/Realization:

Broken hearts can be mended

You have unexpected inner resources to deal with disaster

This, too, shall pass

Life is richer than you ever thought possible

Faint heart never won fair lady

PLOT

Ordinary World:

Always a bridesmaid, never a bride (always second best)

Living without love

Feeling sorry for yourself because of heartbreak

Carefree and heart-whole

Living with constant heartbreak

Trigger Event/Change of Plans:

Losing a loved one

Losing your job or social position

Failing to achieve your goal

Catastrophic illness
Being dumped

Black Moment:

You're about to lose what you love most
To achieve your goal, there is a heavy price to pay
Achieving your goal will break another's heart
A decision breaks your heart
You have to give up what you love most

Resolution:

You decide to sever an unhealthy relationship
You lose the one thing you've always wanted
Something better takes the place of what was lost
You sacrifice one thing but get another
Another's heartbreak gives you success

7◆ – HONOR

CHARACTER

Role/Pursuit: Aristocrat, champion, chevalier, confidante, cowboy, criminal, deserter, fink, guardian, gentleman, heel, hero, informant, knight, lady, military officer, native American, noble, patriot, protector, quitter, samurai, snitch, soldier, statesman, traitor

Trait: Honorable, honest, gallant, truthful, noble, dutiful, distinguished, heroic, dignified, courtly, chivalrous, trustworthy, principled, incorruptible, reliable, corrupt, dishonorable, shameless, disgraced, cowardly, treasonous

Goal/Motivation:
Regain lost honor
Redeem the honor of another
Find honor and glory
Prove another is dishonorable
Guard your honor or another's

Internal Conflict:

The honorable course is a repugnant choice

Saving face is all important

You are too ashamed to act

Cannot stomach the thought of losing honor

Dishonor seems to be the only possible course of action

External Conflict:

You are disgraced by another

You are accused of being a traitor

Your honor is held in contempt

Your actions are perceived to be dishonorable

You dishonor another with your actions

Growth/Realization:

There is honor even among thieves

It is better to die with honor than live with disgrace

Chivalry is not dead

Sometimes you must sacrifice honor to survive

Public glory isn't as important as private honor

PLOT

Ordinary World:

Valuing honor above all else—incorruptible

Dead to all honor

Protecting the honor of family and loved ones

Seeking honor and glory

Living under a cloud of disgrace

Trigger Event/Change of Plans:

A deserter disrupts your life

You are given the opportunity to redeem your honor

Your honor is called into question

The honor of your family is smirched
You receive a call to glory

Black Moment:
The honorable choice will hurt someone you care about
No honorable avenue remains
To achieve your goal, you must sacrifice honor
You are no longer revered
Others receive the honors you deserve

Resolution:
Doing the honorable thing brings success
Making the right choice restores your honor
Another's dishonor is exposed
Regaining honor brings a sense of pride and self-worth
You survived though you had to sacrifice a bit of honor

8 ◆ – IMPROVEMENT

CHARACTER

Role/Pursuit: Athlete, benefactor, body builder, chef, contractor, dieter, dresser, editor, fashion slave, gold digger, hair stylist, healer, humanitarian, image consultant, legislator, maid, make-up artist, mechanic, mentor, painter, pharmacist, photographer, plastic surgeon, psychotherapist, reformer, remodeler, research scientist, self-improvement guru, teacher, test pilot, trainer

Trait: Progressive, improving, forward-looking, helpful, growing, refined, self-confident, goal-oriented, charitable, altruistic, perfecting, overweight, anorexic, insecure, self-conscious, self-critical, uncaring, lazy, unconcerned

Goal/Motivation:
Improve your appearance
Improve your inner self
Help others improve themselves
Make improvements to an organization or institution

Stop improvements from being made

Internal Conflict:
You need improvement
Can't figure out how to improve your situation
Don't see the need for improvement
Improvement requires too much effort
Self-improvement efforts are futile

External Conflict:
Others are trying to improve you
Improvement is too costly
Others' improvements affect you adversely
Others require you to improve yourself
Improvements are halted

Growth/Realization:
The biggest room in the world is the room for improvement
No matter how much you improve yourself, it will never be enough for some people
Self-help is the best help
If it ain't broke, don't fix it
If you aren't part of the solution, you're part of the problem

PLOT

Ordinary World:
Continually trying to improve yourself
Helping others improve themselves
Agitating for improvement
Needing improvement but not knowing how to get it
Refusing to better yourself

Trigger Event/Change of Plans:

You are given an ultimatum to improve or else
You decide to improve yourself
An improvement makes a big change in your life
You discover a way to make a big improvement on something
Improvement suddenly ceases

Black Moment:

All your improvements have been for naught
You realize you will never get better than you are now
Improvements in one area will bring disaster in another
Too much improvement is devastating
Now that things have improved, you are bereft without a goal

Resolution:

Self-improvement results in self-confidence
Helping others improve brings satisfaction
Making the right choice helps you improve yourself
One small improvement changes your life significantly
Stopping improvement efforts brings you peace

9 ◈ – INHERITANCE

CHARACTER

Role/Pursuit: Beneficiary, deputy, executor, farmer, first born, heiress, heir apparent, illegitimate child, ingrate, lady in waiting, lawyer, legatee, noble, prince, prodigal, scion, second in command, successor, understudy, usurper, ward

Trait: Accepting, expectant, pregnant, patient, welcoming, embracing, carefree, deserving, dependent, powerless, unsatisfied, taking, grasping, ungrateful, acquisitive, wasteful, materialistic, abusive, cursed, doomed

Goal/Motivation:
Prove you are the rightful heir
Fulfill the terms of a will to gain inheritance
Get rid of an unwanted inheritance
Learn the details of a genetic inheritance
Prove another incompetent to gain inheritance

Internal Conflict:
You are afraid inheritance will change you
You fear you have inherited a curse
You fear you have inherited a parent's weakness
You fear you are valued only for your inheritance
You place too much dependence on an inheritance

External Conflict:
Someone tries to have you declared incompetent
You are courted solely for your inheritance
Being a beneficiary puts your life in danger
The constraints of inheritance are stifling
Someone else is considered to be the true heir

Growth/Realization:
Anticipating inheritance is dangerous
Blood will tell
Inheritance/Bloodlines are not a measure of worth
Friendship is the only true inheritance
You can't get blood out of a turnip

PLOT

Ordinary World:
Living in constant expectation of inheritance
Expected to produce an heir
Searching for a lost heir
Living in fear of assassination by your heirs
Guarding a historic bloodline

Trigger Event/Change of Plans:
You learn you have inherited a genetic defect
The prodigal returns
You inherit something wonderful

You learn of a dangerous legacy
A family curse is revealed

Black Moment:
The inheritance is lost
Action will result in your family being cursed forever
Your loved ones will inherit your shame
The wrong person is about to inherit the prize
An inheritance puts your life in danger

Resolution:
You inherit self-confidence from the situation
An inheritance gives you the ability to succeed
Giving up your inheritance brings relief
Finding the rightful heir averts misfortune
Learning the truth about your ancestors sets you free

10◆ – INNOCENCE

CHARACTER

Role/Pursuit: Babe in the woods, child, chump, fool, greenhorn, harlot, hayseed, ingénue, innocent, maiden, mark, monk, neophyte, newcomer, novitiate, nun, rogue, rookie, rube, rustic, sacrifice, simpleton, spinster, sucker, tourist, virgin, youngster

Trait: Innocent, virtuous, impressionable, guileless, celibate, childlike, sweet, jejune, idealistic, moral, ignorant, gullible, handicapped, unworldly, vulnerable, naive, clueless, unschooled, defiled, fallen, debauched, sleazy, depraved, wicked, corrupt, violated

Goal/Motivation:
Lose your innocence
Maintain or regain your innocence
Prove your innocence
Assist the world with a return to innocence
Educate an innocent

Internal Conflict:
You fear losing your innocence
Innocence makes you vulnerable
You are too gullible
Your innocence is lost forever
Your innocence is a burden

External Conflict:
Your innocence is called into question
An innocent makes you feel corrupt
Someone tries to take your innocence from you
An innocent is threatened
Another tempts you to lose your innocence

Growth/Realization:
Innocence is no protection
Others are not as innocent as they appeared
Innocence isn't all it's cracked up to be
Innocence is the only protection
There's a sucker born every minute

PLOT

Ordinary World:
Ignorant of the world and its ways—unworldly
Helping the innocent
Living a debauched existence
Determined to keep yourself pure
Trying to lose your innocence

Trigger Event/Change of Plans:
Your innocence comes into question
An innocent is violated
Losing your innocence

Someone takes advantage of your innocence
Someone you thought guilty is proven innocent

Black Moment:

You must sacrifice your innocence
To win, an innocent must suffer
Pleading innocence will bring destruction
Your gullibility has brought you to ruin
You are judged guilty

Resolution:

You are proven innocent
Loss of innocence brings knowledge
Protecting the innocent gives you satisfaction
Maintaining your innocence brings relief
Taking another's innocence is proven to be the only course

J◆ – INSANITY

CHARACTER

Role/Pursuit: Addict, alien, Bedlamite, berserker, devotee, ditz, fan, fanatic, fool, jester, jokester, lunatic, madman, maniac, mental patient, psychiatrist, psychologist, psychopath, radical, split personality, therapist, visionary, zealot

Trait: Zany, madcap, original, creative, brilliant, exalted, silly, scatterbrained, forgetful, talkative, foolish, crazy, mad, hyperactive, moody, ill, insane, senile, possessed, capricious, schizophrenic, hysterical, volatile, rabid

Goal/Motivation:
Prove your sanity
Regain your sanity
Learn whether or not you're crazy
Make sense of an insane world
Get help for an insane person

Internal Conflict:

You fear insanity is hereditary
Fear of losing your sanity
Too flighty to concentrate
You are losing your mental faculties
You suspect you're becoming insane

External Conflict:

Someone is trying to make you insane
Dealing with a scatterbrain is difficult
A loved one shows signs of insanity
Everyone around you appears insane
Someone questions your sanity

Growth/Realization:

Grounding yourself in reality is the only way to maintain sanity
Sanity is an illusion
Insanity is not hereditary
Sanity is overrated
A temporary loss of sanity doesn't make you crazy

PLOT

Ordinary World:

Living in an insane world
Treated as though you are witless
Helping the insane to cope
Constantly in fear of losing your grip on reality
Living in a different reality than everyone else

Trigger Event/Change of Plans:

The world suddenly goes insane
Your sanity is questioned
Losing all grip on reality

A loved one acts insane
A personality splits

Black Moment:
The only course of action will cost you your sanity
You lose your sanity and go berserk
Your actions will cause another to lose sanity
Sudden sanity makes you realize you've been wrong all along
Giving in to insanity is incredibly appealing

Resolution:
Another is proven insane
Sanity is restored, bringing peace
Regaining touch with reality brings success
Remaining sane is the only way to win
A seemingly insane act buys victory

Q♦ – JOY

CHARACTER

Role/Pursuit: Athlete, cartoonist, clown, comic, connoisseur, courtesan, donor, friend, geisha, gigolo, gourmand, hobbyist, humorist, innocent, jester, musician, nymph, parent, peacemaker, philanthropist, practical joker, satyr, toy maker, victor, winner, wit

Trait: Fun-loving, joyous, enthusiastic, cheerful, witty, funny, flamboyant, sensual, impish, gay, impulsive, optimistic, rapt, ecstatic, kind, charitable, unworldly, high-strung, emotional, manic, frenzied

Goal/Motivation:
Find joy in life
Help others find joy
Share your joy with another
Find the humor in the situation
Hide your joy from those who wouldn't understand

Internal Conflict:

There's no joy in your life
An excess of optimism brings disappointment
It's difficult to mask your enthusiasm
Unable to share another's joy
Joy makes you blind to others' faults

External Conflict:

Someone's actions kill your joy
Your enthusiasm is not appreciated
Someone else's joy affects you adversely
Someone tries to put a damper on your joy
Drugs or deception bring false joy

Growth/Realization:

Shared joys are doubled, shared sorrows are halved
You must take time out for fun
Joy is fleeting, so revel in the moment
Joy comes in the small pleasures of life
There is joy in moderation

PLOT

Ordinary World:

You are on top of the world
You experience joy in every aspect of life
You lead a joyless existence
You try to provide joy to everyone else
In constant pursuit of joy

Trigger Event/Change of Plans:

A joyful event brings change
An intended joke goes awry
Sudden loss of joy

A joyful person enters your life
You are fed up with a killjoy

Black Moment:
The loss of joy is devastating
Your joy is based on false assumptions
To win, you must kill another's joy
Life is bleak and joyless
You are no longer having fun

Resolution:
Giving another joy brings you happiness
An unexpected event brings you joy
Finding what really makes you happy gives you joy
Seeing another's joy is all the reward you need
Joyful moments make life worth living

K ◈ – JUDGMENT

CHARACTER

Role/Pursuit: Analyst, appraiser, arbiter, bard, commentator, confessor, critic, deity, editor, executioner, gossip, judge, jury member, law enforcer, lawyer, magistrate, mediator, minister, public defender, referee, reviewer, scientist, tax assessor, umpire, witness

Trait: Analytical, determined, fair, discerning, just, equitable, impartial, balanced, compassionate, dignified, open-minded, listener, sensible, shrewd, intelligent, nonjudgmental, patient, objective, practical, realistic, fair, cautious, judgmental, stubborn, subjective, worrier, fatalistic, doomed, arbitrary, outcast

Goal/Motivation:
Escape judgment
Find justice
Obtain a favorable judgment

Ensure others get their just desserts
Make the correct judgment

Internal Conflict:
It is difficult to be impartial
Can't judge between two options
You fear retribution
You made a bad call
Unable to trust your own judgment

External Conflict:
Justice is not served
Someone misjudges you or your intentions
Someone's poor judgment leaves you in the lurch
There is no appeal for an invalid judgment
You are hounded for an incorrect judgment

Growth/Realization:
Do unto others as you would have them do unto you
Judge not, lest you be judged
You can't judge others by yourself
One person's justice is another's injustice
If you want justice, you have to find it yourself

PLOT

Ordinary World:
Having poor judgment
Sitting in judgment on others
Being the victim of injustice
Seeking justice
Others sit in perpetual judgment on everything you do

Trigger Event/Change of Plans:

Exercising poor judgment leads to major problems
You are shocked by an unjust act
You receive a poor performance evaluation
A verdict goes against you
A judgment comes down in your favor

Black Moment:
A mockery of justice upsets all your plans
Bad judgment threatens ruination
Obtaining justice will destroy everything
Your opponent escapes justice once again
Another's judgment leaves you helpless

Resolution:
Winning a hoped-for judgment brings happiness
Justice triumphs in a way you didn't think possible
Another's poor judgment gives you the edge you need
Though justice is not served, you are satisfied with the outcome
Your correct judgment brings success

PART 4

THE CARDS—SPADES

A♠ – KNOWLEDGE

CHARACTER

Role/Pursuit: Academic, advisor, aesthete, amnesiac, authority, bookseller, consultant, egghead, elder, expert, explorer, fool, genius, graduate, guide, guru, highbrow, honor student, know-it-all, master, mentor, originator, Ph.D., professional, professor, protégé, researcher, savage, savant, scholar, scientist, statistician, teacher, trivia buff, wise one

Trait: Intellectual, intelligent, skilled, discerning, literate, clever, wise, omniscient, photographic memory, educated, experienced, knowledgeable, ingenious, worldly, bookish, studious, aloof, forgetful, ignorant, wordy, illiterate, backward, primitive, uncivilized

Goal/Motivation:
Protect valuable knowledge or information
Acquire knowledge or a piece of information
Contribute to the world's knowledge
Eliminate someone's knowledge

Help others acquire knowledge

Internal Conflict:
You have amnesia or can't remember something important
You are burdened with too much knowledge
You are illiterate
You don't have enough knowledge or information
Your knowledge is dangerous

External Conflict:
The world isn't ready for your knowledge
Others forcibly demand your knowledge
Your knowledge is challenged or repudiated
Others demand the source of your confidential information
Others think you have information you don't possess

Growth/Realization:
Knowledge is power
Having knowledge is not the same as possessing wisdom
It's not what you know that counts, but how you use it
What they don't know won't hurt them
You must listen to your feelings, not just your intellect

PLOT

Ordinary World:
Living in an academic environment
Secure and/or smug in your own knowledge
Feeling ignorant or unable to remember
Living in a sea of information
Striving to learn as much as possible

Trigger Event/Change of Plans:
A scientific experiment goes awry

You acquire a shocking piece of knowledge
Someone offers to sell you information
You lose your memory or forgotten memories resurface
Others force unwanted knowledge upon you

Black Moment:
Valuable knowledge is about to be lost forever
Too much knowledge has placed you in a dangerous position
Your lack of knowledge is about to cause disaster
You have forgotten something vital
Gaining forbidden knowledge is devastating

Resolution:
Deciding not to press for dangerous knowledge brings relief
Selective amnesia is best for all concerned
The acquisition of knowledge brings success
Sharing information with the world helps share the burden
It's not what you know, but who you know that helps you win

2♠ – LONELINESS

CHARACTER

Role/Pursuit: Astronaut, bachelor, bookworm, castaway, drifter, expatriate, fugitive, hermit, hobo, inmate, loner, lumberjack, miner, miser, monk, outcast, outlaw, pariah, pioneer, recluse, refugee, runaway, scout, shut-in, spinster, writer

Trait: Searching, serene, individual, solitary, detached, expatriate, single, uninvolved, isolated, withdrawn, childless, cool, abandoned, separated, forsaken, alienated, lonely, friendless, unsociable, fearful, untrusting, selfish

Goal/Motivation:
Be left alone
End your loneliness
Isolate another
Rejoin society
Help the lonely

Internal Conflict:
Fear of living alone the rest of your life
Frightened of people or crowds
Fed up with being alone
Lonely even in a crowd
Being lonely is better than being hurt again

External Conflict:
You are abandoned by another
Your solitary life is threatened
Separated from loved ones
Forced isolation makes you lonely
Others are forbidden to end your loneliness

Growth/Realization:
You cannot live by bread alone
Being in any kind of relationship is better than being alone
It is better to be alone than in bad company
Being alone doesn't mean you're lonely
Choosing to be alone is not a sin

PLOT

Ordinary World:
Living in loneliness
Living a happy, solitary existence
Outcast from society
Making sure you are never alone
Seeking solitude

Trigger Event/Change of Plans:
You are suddenly alone for the first time in your life
You are declared an outcast
Your loneliness is abruptly ended

You decide to end another's loneliness
Another's departure brings loneliness

Black Moment:

The right choice will make you forever outcast
The fruition of your plans brings utter loneliness
Your prized solitude is shattered forever
Your action will doom another to loneliness
You will never be left alone again

Resolution:

The right choice brings the end of loneliness
You finally find blessed solitude
Though you are lonely now, you know it won't last forever
Ending another's loneliness brings satisfaction
You choose to be alone, bringing relief

3♠ – LOVE

CHARACTER

Role/Pursuit: Bride, coquette, courtier, cupid, Don Juan, duenna, father, flirt, gallant, groom, husband, idol, jilt, lecher, lover, matchmaker, mistress, mother, nymph, pimp, playboy, prostitute, rake, relationship counselor, satyr, soul mate, vamp, wedding planner, wife

Trait: Affectionate, selfless, devoted, loving, romantic, caring, charitable, doting, flirtatious, worshipping, coy, amorous, ardent, passionate, teasing, jealous, possessive, clinging, hateful, lecherous, adulterous, vengeful

Goal/Motivation:
Find a lasting, loving relationship
Help others find love
Find a lost love
Repair a broken relationship
Discover passion

Internal Conflict:

Afraid of passion or making love

Fear of commitment

Feeling you don't deserve love or don't know how to love

Feeling overwhelming jealousy of a loved one

The love in your relationship is missing or lost

External Conflict:

Others find you overly passionate

Someone is trying to make you jealous or take love away

Another's love is unwanted

Your lover is overly possessive

All your attempts at finding love have failed

Growth/Realization:

It's better to have loved and lost than to never have loved at all

Making love is not the same as loving

Love is blind, but neighbors aren't

You can't live on love alone

It is better to love someone you cannot have than to have someone you cannot love

PLOT

Ordinary World:

Surrounded by love

Unable to find love

Love 'em and leave 'em

Hounded by unwanted or inconvenient love

Playing at love

Trigger Event/Change of Plans:

Falling in love

A declaration of love catches you off-guard

You are possessed by jealousy
Love dies
Making love changes everything

Black Moment:
Learning the one you love will never love you
Making love or being in love is no longer enjoyable
Your actions have cost you love
You will never love again
Love brings despair

Resolution:
Believing in love brings success
The right choice brings unexpected love
Love begets forgiveness
Sharing unconditional love brings happiness
Doing the right thing helps you regain love

4♠ – LOYALTY

CHARACTER

Role/Pursuit: Armsman, champion, chauvinist, crusader, cultist, defector, double agent, friend, gang member, groupie, guard, handmaiden, henchman, knight, mobster, nationalist, parent, pet, patriot, protector, reformer, squire, spouse, traitor, turncoat, unionist, vassal, yeoman

Trait: Loyal, faithful, true, selfless, honorable, accommodating, supportive, constant, generous, patriotic, parochial, incorruptible, steady, staunch, sacrificing, sectarian, chauvinistic, prejudiced, faithless, treacherous, traitorous, corrupt, forsworn

Goal/Motivation:
Earn another's loyalty
Prove another's disloyalty
Prove your loyalty
Find who has betrayed you
Find loyalty in something

Internal Conflict:
Loyalty makes you blind to others' faults
Feeling you don't deserve loyalty
Disloyalty lives in your heart
Loyalty is a burden you don't want
Tempted to be disloyal

External Conflict:
Someone's disloyalty is devastating
Your loyalty is called into question
Your loyalty is betrayed
Unwanted loyalty is stifling
Misplaced loyalty brings you grief

Growth/Realization:
You must stand for something
To get loyalty, you must first be loyal
There is no such thing as a small disloyalty
Loyalty determines a person's true worth
Misplaced loyalty is no virtue

PLOT

Ordinary World:
Being utterly loyal
Shunned for disloyalty
Seeking a cause to believe in
Responsible for determining others' loyalty
Seeking true loyalty

Trigger Event/Change of Plans:
You are betrayed by someone you trusted
Your loyalty is tested
Learning your loyalty was given under false pretenses

Receiving unswerving and unexpected loyalty
Your disloyalty is discovered

Black Moment:
You can trust no one's loyalty
Your disloyalty is unmasked
Loyalty is broken forever
Misguided loyalty threatens ruin
Being loyal will cause destruction

Resolution:
Standing by your friends confers success
The right decision brings unexpected loyalty
Disloyalty is unmasked to help you win
In a question of loyalty, you learn who your true friends are
Success shows your loyalty was not misplaced

5♠ – LUCK

CHARACTER

Role/Pursuit: Adventurer, angler, breeder, candidate, card sharp, chosen one, contestant, daredevil, explorer, fraud, gambler, guinea pig, hunter, jinx, leprechaun, miner, oil man, player, pool shark, risk taker, speculator, spy, stock market analyst, stunt man, swindler, test pilot, thrill-seeker, venture capitalist, warrior

Trait: Lucky, fortunate, blessed, charmed, favored, daring, shrewd, prosperous, adventurous, wealthy, speculative, unpredictable, unlucky, rash, disappointed, ill-fated, snakebit, foolhardy, calamity-prone, reckless, cursed, jinxed, hexed

Goal/Motivation:
Test your luck
Get past an unlucky streak
Take advantage of a run of luck
Learn the details of a curse
Rid yourself or another of a jinx or curse

Internal Conflict:
You are unlucky
Don't want to test your luck
You feel like a jinx
A run of luck makes you reckless
Your luck is unpredictable

External Conflict:
You are cursed by another
You can't win against another's phenomenal luck
Your luck is thwarted by a jinx
You have a string of bad luck
Someone is trying to end your string of luck

Growth/Realization:
Pressing your luck can be dangerous
Luck is always against the one who depends upon it
The only sure thing about luck is that it is bound to change
It is better to be lucky than skilled
Curses rebound threefold upon the curser

PLOT

Ordinary World:
The victim of a string of bad luck
A run of good luck has put you on top of the world
Living on luck
Dealing with someone who is addicted to gambling
Working in a gaming establishment

Trigger Event/Change of Plans:
Your luck suddenly changes
You win an unexpected prize
You become the victim of a strong curse

Someone decides you are a lucky charm
You become the object of a wager

Black Moment:
You can't count on luck to get you out of a bad situation
The only kind of luck you have is bad
The outcome is dependent on the results of a wild gamble
You gambled and lost, so must now face the consequences
Your luck fails when you need it most

Resolution:
A lucky event gives you what you need to succeed
A gamble pays off
Relying on skill rather than luck brings success
Breaking a curse brings relief
Another's bad luck is your good luck

6♠ – MAGIC

CHARACTER

Role/Pursuit: Adept, astrologist, believer, dreamer, druid, elf, enchantress, fairy creature, fairy godmother, familiar, genie, imp, mage, magician's assistant, miracle-worker, necromancer, shaman, shapeshifter, sorceress, spell caster, voodooist, witch, wizard

Trait: Magical, fey, elfin, otherworldly, revered, whimsical, charming, mythical, bewitching, impish, spellbinding, supernatural, elusive, imaginative, enchanting, enthralled, spellbound, puckish, superior, godlike, diabolical, distrusting

Goal/Motivation:
Find magic in your life
Discover the secrets of magic
Create something magical
Enchant someone
Help others discover magic

Internal Conflict:
Don't believe in magic or miracles
There's no magic in your life
Can't believe in anything
Unable to conceive of anything magical or whimsical
Don't believe in your own power

External Conflict:
The magic is fading or has disappeared
Others doubt your magic
You are spellbound by another
Your magic is unpredictable
Magic has let you down

Growth/Realization:
Magic has a price
The world is too mundane without magic
You have to make miracles happen yourself
You are the source of all magic
Magic is overrated

PLOT

Ordinary World:
Engrossed in the study of magic
Debunking claims of magic
Searching for magic
Surrounded by magic
Living a life devoid of magic or miracles

Trigger Event/Change of Plans:
You experience a truly magical moment
You learn you have a fairy godmother
You acquire an object with reputed magical powers

The magic is lost
You suddenly gain powers

Black Moment:
The magic is gone forever
The miracle you hoped for doesn't arrive
Your magic is turned against you
You no longer believe in anything
The magic was an illusion

Resolution:
Making the right decision helps you find magic
You find the magic within yourself to achieve success
Eschewing magic for reality brings wisdom
Believing in magic brings hope
With wisdom, you are able to see the magic around you

7♠ – MISFIT

CHARACTER

Role/Pursuit: Alien, black sheep, bohemian, character, crackpot, eccentric, ex-con, fish out of water, flake, foreigner, freak, geek, heretic, homosexual, lone wolf, maverick, misfit, mongrel, mutt, nerd, newcomer, nonconformist, oddball, oddity, outsider, rookie, scapegoat, screwball, sociopath, wallflower

Trait: Unorthodox, unique, reserved, quiet, unusual, offbeat, solitary, original, shy, unconventional, different, idiosyncratic, quaint, whimsical, quirky, flaky, eccentric, lonely, handicapped, weird, odd, abnormal, deviant, ugly

Goal/Motivation:
Find a place where you will fit in
Join a popular clique
Make others accept you as you are
Change yourself so you won't be considered odd
Follow a different drummer

Internal Conflict:
Feel as though you don't fit in
Embarrassed by your own or another's eccentricities
Not wanting to conform or follow the rules
Being unconventional gives you guilty pleasure
Hating the thought of being considered different

External Conflict:
Ostracized for being different
Others try to make you conform
Condemned for your idiosyncrasies
Forced into a role that is a bad fit for your personality
Your individuality is forcibly suppressed

Growth/Realization:
You are known by the company you keep
You shouldn't try to be something you're not
True friends accept you even with your idiosyncrasies
Diversity should be celebrated, not denigrated
Conforming is not the same as fitting in

PLOT

Ordinary World:
Being an outsider or misfit
Constantly trying to conform to others' standards
Not realizing you are different from everyone else
Seeking some place to fit in
Subject to unrelenting peer pressure

Trigger Event/Change of Plans:
Moving to a new location makes you feel like an outsider
Finding a place to fit in
Rejecting imposed standards

Learning you are different
Ostracized for being different

Black Moment:
Success will make you a misfit forever
Forced conformity will take away your identity
Your differences are exposed, bringing ostracism
Prejudice makes you a victim
Your prejudice threatens failure

Resolution:
Being yourself leads to success
Breaking the shackles of conformity brings relief
Accepting others as they are creates a win-win situation
Finally finding a place to fit in brings happiness
Celebrating your difference gives you joy

8♠ – POWER

CHARACTER

Role/Pursuit: Boxer, bully, chancellor, chief, commander, committee chair, delegate, dictator, electrician, executive, inquisitor, leader, manager, master, nobleman, overlord, political candidate, politician, president, regent, ringleader, royalty, sorceress, statesman, taskmaster, victim, warden, wizard, wrestler

Trait: Charismatic, charming, magnetic, powerful, invincible, energetic, dynamic, decisive, savvy, bold, ambitious, vigorous, forceful, intense, swaggering, aggressive, powerless, dominating, overwhelming, weak, ineffective, smarmy, corrupt, power-hungry

Goal/Motivation:
Overthrow another's power
Find the power to change
Gain power over others
Use power to advantage
Escape the yoke of power

Internal Conflict:

Powerless to change
Secretly crave power
Overly ambitious
Corrupted by power
Lacking the power to succeed

External Conflict:

Others have too much power over you
Someone is trying to undermine your power
Your power base is threatened
You are overpowered by another
Others credit you with too much power

Growth/Realization:

Power corrupts
Power finds its own level
To have what you want is riches, but to do without is power
Vanity made you overestimate your power
Power is the ultimate reward

PLOT

Ordinary World:

Powerless and victimized
In a position of unassailable power
Seeking power
Trying to undermine or overthrow another's power
Using power wisely

Trigger Event/Change of Plans:

A sudden power shift changes everything
You are cut off from your source of power
You or a loved one are overpowered

You suddenly feel empowered
Power is forced upon you

Black Moment:
Faced with a complete loss of power
The only solution requires a gross misuse of power
A bully is about to win
To win, you must give up power
You are powerless and helpless

Resolution:
Doing the right thing empowers you
Sharing power brings success
Exercising power wisely brings contentment
Giving up power brings relief
Success brings power

9♠ – PRIDE

CHARACTER

Role/Pursuit: Aristocrat, artist, athlete, author, blowhard, braggart, coxcomb, champion, craftsman, egotist, inventor, movie star, parent, peacock, phony, prima donna, professional, royalty, showoff, snob, socialite, statesman, victor, winner

Trait: Confident, upstanding, noble, proud, distinguished, humble, regal, satisfied, dignified, self- assured, complacent, headstrong, elitist, meek, insecure, uppity, presumptuous, conceited, arrogant, haughty, puffed up, vain, patronizing, egocentric, self-centered

Goal/Motivation:
Earn someone's pride
Have pride in yourself
Be proud of another
Puncture false pride
Find humility

Internal Conflict:
Too proud to accept help
Have no pride to speak of
Pride leads you into trouble
A lack of pride in yourself
Pride is costing you happiness

External Conflict:
Others undermine your pride
Others scoff at your pride and joy
Pride in the group requires you to do something you'd rather not
Others find your pride insufferable
You lose pride in another

Growth/Realization:
Pride goes before a fall
Humility is the foundation of all virtues
Pride is a luxury you can't afford
Pride won't keep you warm
Feeling proud of yourself is worth the cost

PLOT

Ordinary World:
Trying to keep up with the Joneses
Proud of your accomplishments
Feeling a lack of pride in anything
Teaching others to be proud
Overly prideful

Trigger Event/Change of Plans:
Someone does you proud
You are humiliated
You feel proud for the first time in your life

Your pride goes out the window
Another's overweening pride affects your life

Black Moment:
Your pride is shattered
Overweening pride brings disaster
To win, you must destroy another's pride
Lost pride is humiliating
Learning your pride is false

Resolution:
Doing the right thing makes you proud of yourself
Keeping pride in check leads to success
Regaining pride in yourself is priceless
Being proud of another is as satisfying as pride in yourself
Learning true humility is rewarding

10♠ – QUENCH

CHARACTER

Role/Pursuit: Baker, bartender, caterer, chef, drug dealer, epicure, gigolo, gourmand, grocer, lender, masseuse, nymph, pharmacist, playboy, pleasure-seeker, prostitute, rake, restaurateur, satyr, swinger, sybarite, tease, waitress

Trait: Satisfied, fulfilled, content, eager, avid, thirsty, hungry, anxious, sensual, impatient, raving, spoiled, hard-pressed, self-indulgent, quelling, obsessed, fixated, hedonistic, gluttonous, insatiable, rapacious, greedy

Goal/Motivation:
Satisfy an appetite or quench a thirst for something
Walk on the wild side
Obtain satisfaction for a wrong
Help others satisfy their appetites
Indulge your senses for once

Internal Conflict:
A tendency to overindulge your senses
Satisfying your appetites feels wrong
You are never satisfied
You are spoiled
You feel a lack of sensuality

External Conflict:
Others dismiss you as a spoiled brat
Others force their appetites upon you
Others disapprove of your sensuality
Your self-indulgence hurts others
Forced to indulge your senses

Growth/Realization:
Pouring oil on the fire is not the way to quench it
Moderation is the best means
There is more joy in anticipation than realization
The grass is always greener on the other side
Indulging in a little satisfaction doesn't make you a bad person

PLOT

Ordinary World:
Spoiled and indulged by your loved ones
Happily self-indulgent
Never satisfied with what you have
Unable to achieve satisfaction
Helping others achieve satisfaction

Trigger Event/Change of Plans:
You decide to quench a thirst or appetite
Your indulgence comes to an end
You realize you aren't satisfied with your life

You realize your appetite is out of control
You decide to have one last fling

Black Moment:
The fire is quenched forever
You realize you will never be satisfied
Achieving satisfaction will bring disaster
Quenching your appetite will hurt another
Spoiling another brings ruination

Resolution:
Indulging a craving brings satisfaction
Abstinence is its own reward
Achieving satisfaction is worth it
Achieving moderation brings relief
Slaking an appetite once is all it takes to satisfy you

J♠ – RESCUE

CHARACTER

Role/Pursuit: Bodyguard, captive, champion, commando, defender, firefighter, guard, guardian, hero, hijacker, keeper, kidnapper, knight, mountie, parent, pirate, police officer, prisoner, savior, search and rescue, social worker, tracker, warrior, watchman

Trait: Caring, humane, helpful, brave, chivalrous, daring, bold, protective, tenacious, adventurous, solicitous, determined, opportunistic, responsible, worried, fearful, vulnerable, overprotective, defenseless

Goal/Motivation:
Be rescued
Rescue yourself or another
Defend yourself or another from harm
Keep someone safe
Ensure there is no chance of rescue

Internal Conflict:
Don't feel worthy of rescue
Doubt your ability to save another
Rely too much on others to rescue you
You don't want to be saved
Tired of constantly coming to the rescue

External Conflict:
You are an unwilling captive
There is no chance of rescue
Rescue comes with a steep price attached
You are unable to effect a rescue
Someone insists on rescuing you despite your protests

Growth/Realization:
If you want to be rescued, you have to do it yourself
You are in a prison of your own making
You must let your guard down sometime
Walls do not make a prison
Rescue isn't all it's cracked up to be

PLOT

Ordinary World:
Held captive
Dedicated to saving others
In constant need of rescue
Guarding others from escape or capture
Arranging the rescue of others

Trigger Event/Change of Plans:
You are held captive
A loved one is in need of rescue
A rescue attempt is bungled

A criminal escapes
A rescue attempt succeeds

Black Moment:
The rescue attempt fails
The captive doesn't want to be rescued
There is no chance of rescue
Attempted rescue will increase the danger
Your opponent escapes your trap

Resolution:
Rescuing another brings pride and satisfaction
Saving yourself brings pride and satisfaction
There is no need for rescue, bringing relief
The villain is recaptured, bringing safety
You are saved

Q♠ – REVENGE

CHARACTER

Role/Pursuit: Bully, casualty, demotee, deposed leader, displaced heir, injured party, innocent, jilt, law enforcer, mark, nemesis, prison guard, prisoner, resistance fighter, scapegoat, traitor, undercover worker, victim, vigilante

Trait: Just, righteous, intense, determined, resolute, complex, unwavering, deep, unswerving, resentful, injured, damaging, embarrassed, spiteful, angry, vindictive, punishing, malevolent, retaliatory, bitter, victimized, wounded, obsessed

Goal/Motivation:
Ensure others get their just deserts
Pay off an old score and/or get revenge
Escape revenge
Turn the tables on another
Deal with the consequences of revenge

Internal Conflict:
Thoughts of revenge cloud your judgment and make you bitter
Feeling guilty about your need for revenge
Seeking revenge threatens your way of life
Don't know why others seek revenge against you
Don't know how to get revenge

External Conflict:
Others seek revenge against you
Others cause you to seek revenge
Unable to get revenge
Others block you from getting revenge
Cannot locate the object of your revenge

Growth/Realization:
The best revenge is living well
Those who insist on an eye for an eye lack vision
Revenge is a dish best served cold
Revenge is sweet
The noblest revenge is forgiveness

PLOT

Ordinary World:
Seeking vengeance
Helping others find vengeance
Bitter about unfulfilled revenge
Living in the midst of a feud
Keeping others from seeking revenge

Trigger Event/Change of Plans:
You are suddenly presented with the means for revenge
A heinous act makes you seek revenge
Others declare vengeance upon you

A feud escalates rapidly
Sudden fulfillment of vengeance leaves you without purpose

Black Moment:

You must live with the consequences of your acts
The results of revenge are impossible to live with
Revenge does not bring satisfaction or freedom from pain
Getting revenge is a double-edged sword
Achieving revenge merely begets another cycle of feuding

Resolution:

You give up your need for revenge, bringing closure
The tables are turned, bringing sweet revenge
An ironic revenge brings satisfaction
The fulfillment of revenge allows you to get on with your life
A loved one is avenged, bringing justice

K♠ – RICHES

CHARACTER

Role/Pursuit: Accountant, banker, beggar, benefactor, broker, collector, creditor, economist, financier, gambler, gold digger, gold miner, investor, jeweler, landowner, Midas, millionaire, miser, pauper, rag picker, ruler, scrooge, shareholder, stockbroker, tax collector, treasure hunter, treasurer

Trait: Generous, benevolent, wealthy, opportunistic, unselfish, wise, charitable, prudent, prosperous, lavish, valuable, thrifty, knowledgeable, extravagant, unappreciative, materialistic, poor, unworthy, needy, spendthrift, undeserving, bankrupt, stingy, cheap

Goal/Motivation:
Acquire wealth
Gain financial backing
Share the wealth
Get rid of an embarrassment of riches
Help yourself or another find treasure

Internal Conflict:

Money is a burden, not a pleasure
Don't have enough money
You are overly generous
You are too stingy or cheap
You resent another's benevolence or charity

External Conflict:

Someone tries to take away your riches
Unable to get financial assistance
Another's excessive generosity is oppressive
Faced with repayment of a large loan
Unable to locate or access your money

Growth/Realization:

Money can't buy happiness
Riches and care are inseparable
Riches, like manure, do no good unless they are spread around
Riches make friends, and adversity proves them
The lack of money is the root of all evil

PLOT

Ordinary World:

Living in the lap of luxury
Living in poverty or ever-mounting debt
In constant pursuit of riches
Playing Robin Hood
Living on another's generosity

Trigger Event/Change of Plans:

You lose money
Something valuable is missing
A creditor calls in a debt immediately

You learn the location of hidden treasure
You suddenly acquire riches

Black Moment:
You are utterly bankrupt
Hordes of money-hungry parasites descend upon you
Riches make you unable to tell friend from foe
Someone else gets the treasure
What you valued most is gone forever

Resolution:
Money arrives from an unexpected source when you need it most
Loss of riches helps you realize who your true friends are
Sharing the wealth brings satisfaction
Finding the treasure brings success
Another's generosity gives you the ability to succeed

PART 5

THE CARDS—HEARTS

A ♥ – SACRIFICE

CHARACTER

Role/Pursuit: Assassin, athlete, bodyguard, care provider, devil, donor, fool, hatchet man, holy person, martyr, masochist, monk, parent, ritual murderer, nun, patsy, prey, priestess, quarry, sacrifice, saint, scapegoat, victim, virgin, volunteer, witch

Trait: Idealistic, giving, saintly, self-sacrificing, patient, unselfish, charitable, abstinent, celibate, innocent, controlled, penitent, temperate, atoning, repentant, martyred, suffering, tortured, despairing, desperate, murderous

Goal/Motivation:
Avoid sacrifice
Find a substitute sacrifice
Offer yourself in another's place
Sacrifice one thing to gain another
Learn what a sacrifice entails

Internal Conflict:

Unwilling to sacrifice
Feeling like a martyr
Too self-sacrificing
Unsure if sacrifice is worth it
Sacrifice has become a dreaded way of life

External Conflict:

Others don't appreciate your sacrifice
You are expected to sacrifice something you don't want to
You are accused of acting like a martyr
You are the sacrifice
You are pressured by another's sacrifice

Growth/Realization:

Sacrificing yourself for another is the ultimate satisfaction
Self-sacrifice builds character
The only thing you can't sacrifice is your self-respect
There is no honor in grudging sacrifice
Continued sacrifice is unnecessary

PLOT

Ordinary World:

Sacrifice is your way of life
Living with a martyr
Living with the consequences of another's sacrifice
Prepared to offer yourself as a sacrifice
Refusing to sacrifice anything

Trigger Event/Change of Plans:

You are offered up as the sacrificial lamb or scapegoat
Your sacrifice is rejected
A sacrifice is demanded of you

You learn of an impending sacrifice
Another's sacrifice catches you by surprise

Black Moment:
Your sacrifice is meaningless
To succeed, you must sacrifice something precious
No sacrifice will ever be enough
You must sacrifice everything you hold dear
Despite your best efforts, the sacrifice will proceed

Resolution:
Sacrificing yourself for another brings success
Self-sacrifice brings wisdom
Averting an unnecessary sacrifice helps you win
The right decision brings the end of sacrifice
Your sacrifice is not in vain

2♥ – SECRETS

CHARACTER

Role/Pursuit: Biographer, busybody, celebrity, confessor, confidante, counselor, detective, eavesdropper, explorer, gossip columnist, homosexual, informant, investigative reporter, secret agent, snoop, spy, tattletale, traitor, treasure hunter, undercover work

Trait: Secretive, private, close-mouthed, tightlipped, mysterious, taciturn, gossipy, enigmatic, cryptic, sly, furtive, tattletale, evasive, devious, scandalmonger, untrusting, fearful, deceptive, underhanded, sneaky, slanderous

Goal/Motivation:
Keep a secret at all costs
Expose a secret
Learn someone else's secret
Hide a secret so no one will find out
Eliminate the need for secrets

Internal Conflict:

Tired of secrets

Unable to keep a secret

Being overly secretive

Afraid to reveal a secret

You want to confess a secret but can't

External Conflict:

Pressured to reveal your secrets

Keeping a promise to maintain a secret causes hardship

Someone reveals your secrets

You are blackmailed

You are burdened with others' secrets

Growth/Realization:

You can't expect others to keep a secret you can't keep yourself

Sharing the secret shares the load

Keeping a secret is no hardship for a true friend

Some secrets are too dangerous to keep

Sometimes exposing a secret is the only way to progress

PLOT

Ordinary World:

Living surrounded by secrets

Make a living exposing secrets

Being the keeper of many secrets

Deriving enjoyment from ferreting out secrets

Unaware of a loved one's secret past

Trigger Event/Change of Plans:

Your secret is exposed

You learn a secret

Something seemingly ordinary is suddenly veiled in secrecy

You are threatened with blackmail
You decide to learn the truth about an intriguing secret

Black Moment:
All your secrets are laid bare
Revealing a secret causes harm to an innocent
Learning a secret is devastating
A secret revealed too early brings your plans to naught
The price of keeping a secret is too high

Resolution:
Exposing a secret clears the air
The right decision keeps your secret safe
Keeping a secret brings success
Sharing a secret brings relief
Another's secret is exposed, bringing you success

3♥ – SELF

CHARACTER

Role/Pursuit: Alzheimer's sufferer, amnesiac, egotist, entrepreneur, ghost, groupie, mental patient, personage, psychiatrist, psychologist, pushover, schizophrenic, sociopath, soloist, spirit, split personality, stroke victim, therapist, wanderer

Trait: Self-confident, self-possessed, self-conscious, unique, self-starter, self-contained, individualistic, self-deprecating, private, self-important, self-satisfied, self-centered, selfish, self-righteous, suicidal, worthless, self-seeking, narcissistic, soulless

Goal/Motivation:
Find yourself
Regain your mental faculties
Keep from losing your sense of self
Find self-confidence
Maintain your privacy

Internal Conflict:
Lack of self-confidence
Lost your sense of self
Overly selfish and/or self-centered
You have no self-control
You dislike your self-image

External Conflict:
Your mental stability is questioned
Your sense of self is attacked
Your individuality is threatened
Can't be yourself around others
Your identity is challenged

Growth/Realization:
Self-conquest is the greatest of all victories
Self-interest is the beginning of wisdom
Self-help is the best kind of help
With self-confidence, half the battle is won
To love others, you must first love yourself

PLOT

Ordinary World:
Self-absorbed
Self-denying
Helping others with identity problems
Seeking your true self
Lacking a sense of self

Trigger Event/Change of Plans:
A personality suddenly changes
Your self-confidence is tested
Realizing you don't know who you are anymore

You lose a piece of yourself
Realizing you don't like what you've become

Black Moment:

Your self-confidence is shattered
Selfish acts have brought ruin
A lack of self-identity leaves you rudderless
Winning will cause you to loathe yourself
Acting self-righteous leaves you alone and friendless

Resolution:

The right decision makes you more self-confident
Self-denial leads to success
Practicing self-control helps you win
Doing the right thing helps you like yourself again
A change in self-image helps you cope

4♥ – SIN

CHARACTER

Role/Pursuit: Adulterer, cannibal, criminal, demon, evangelist, exorcist, gangster, glutton, lawbreaker, lecher, miser, missionary, murderer, nymphomaniac, pimp, preacher, rake, reformer, seducer, teetotaler, temperance advocate, thief, thug

Trait: Passionate, enchanting, abstinent, innocent, sensual, provocative, chaste, pure, ardent, tempting, seductive, proud, kinky, luring, angry, covetous, envious, slothful, wicked, priggish, moral, lustful, dissipated, immoral, sinful, sacrilegious, carnal, debauched, possessed

Goal/Motivation:
Atone for your sins
Be forgiven for your sins
Confess your sins
Drive sin out of others
Sin a little

Internal Conflict:

You feel sinful
A little sin doesn't seem so bad
There is sin in your heart
You secretly want to experience sin
You are ashamed of your sins

External Conflict:

A loved one's sin burdens you
Another threatens to expose your sins
You are accused of a sin you did not commit
You are berated for having a total lack of sin
You are forced into sin

Growth/Realization:

Virtue is its own reward
A sin confessed is half forgiven
If you sin in haste, you will repent at leisure
The wages of sin are too expensive
Sometimes a small sin keeps life on an even keel

PLOT

Ordinary World:

Rooting out sin wherever you find it
Preaching against sin
Living in sin
Trying to destroy yourself in sin
Living a sin-free life

Trigger Event/Change of Plans:

An unexpected event makes you vow to sin no more
Your sin is discovered
Another confesses a sin to you

You are asked to cover up a sin
You are sinned against

Black Moment:

All your sins catch up with you
To win, you must commit a sin
Exposing a sin will hurt another
You discover you are not without sin yourself
The sins of the world are on your shoulders

Resolution:

You are forgiven for your sins
What you thought was a major sin turns out to be a minor peccadillo
Forgiving another's sins leads to harmony
Making the right decision brings forgiveness
Atoning for your sins brings relief

5♥ – SLOTH

CHARACTER

Role/Pursuit: Beachcomber, beggar, bum, drifter, drone, fisherman, gold digger, hanger-on, hypochondriac, idle rich, loafer, loiterer, overlord, panhandler, parasite, pensioner, playboy, remittance man, retired, truant, trust fund recipient, unemployed, vagabond, vagrant, wastrel, welfare recipient

Trait: Lackadaisical, carefree, easygoing, unstressed, idle, bored, unambitious, laissez-faire, slow, dreamy, apathetic, uncommitted, uninvolved, lazy, listless, dawdling, lethargic, lax, slothful, uncaring, stuporous

Goal/Motivation:
Be lazy for a change
Avoid life's responsibilities and stress
Find rest and relaxation after a lifetime of hard work
Get rid of apathy
Make the world go away

Internal Conflict:
Too lazy to change things
Unable to muster enough energy
Dislike having nothing to do
Doing nothing is easier than taking action
Unable to sit still for a minute

External Conflict:
Forced inactivity makes you idle
Thrust into unemployment or retirement
Others try to force you out of your apathy or lethargy
You are derided for your lack of ambition
Another's sloth puts a burden on you

Growth/Realization:
Sloth is the mother of vice
A lazy person works the hardest
A little laziness is good for the soul
Only the wise can employ leisure well
All work and no play makes you a dull person

PLOT

Ordinary World:
Drifting from one place to another
Unemployed or retired
Seeking rest and relaxation
Attempting to put vagrants to work
Unwilling to work

Trigger Event/Change of Plans:
You decide to quit work
You are forcibly retired or unemployed
You are suddenly responsible for a slothful person

You take a vacation from responsibility
You are jolted out of inactivity by an unexpected event

Black Moment:
You decide to give up
Your laziness brings disaster
You are faced with forced inactivity or prison
Apathy makes you unable to act
No one cares about your situation

Resolution:
Overcoming laziness brings self-respect
Winning allows you to live a life of ease
Overcoming apathy leads to a renewed interest in life
Doing nothing is the right decision
Taking a short vacation brings renewed enthusiasm

6♥ – STRENGTH

CHARACTER

Role/Pursuit: Adventurer, athlete, builder, conqueror, coward, expert, giant, hero, laborer, lumberjack, pioneer, pugilist, punk, roustabout, sportsman, stevedore, stud, super hero, victor, Viking, warrior, weakling, weight lifter, weenie, wimp, wrestler

Trait: Strong, powerful, gentle, athletic, resolute, rugged, hearty, worthy, brave, dependable, stable, intense, invulnerable, tough, durable, built to last, heroic, brawny, healthy, solid, enduring, ethical, weak, pathetic, rough, hard, forceful, soft, opinionated, mushy, stubborn, leaky, strong-willed, inflexible

Goal/Motivation:
Find or regain strength
Overcome a weakness
Discover your strengths
Be strong for others
Use your strength wisely

Internal Conflict:

Don't know your own strength

Too weak

Don't have the strength to go on

Too much strength makes you foolhardy

You lack strength of character

External Conflict:

Your opponent is much stronger than you

Your strength has been challenged

Your strength has been taken from you

Others are jealous of your strength

Others misjudge your strength

Growth/Realization:

You are stronger than you ever thought possible

There is strength in numbers

Using your brain is often wiser than depending on your strength

Only the strong survive

Everyone has a weak side

PLOT

Ordinary World:

Others depend on your strength

Trying to build up your strength

Using your strength to make a living

Trying to find your own strengths

Trying to diminish another's strength

Trigger Event/Change of Plans:

Your Achilles heel is discovered

You lose your strength

Your strength is put to the test

Overpowered by another's strength
You gain sudden strength

Black Moment:
Your strength fails
Weakness leads to failure
You can no longer carry the world on your shoulders
You are not strong enough to prevail
Your strength is revealed to be a sham

Resolution:
You find the strength to succeed
Gaining strength of character brings success
Overcoming weakness brings self-respect
Making the right decision gives you the strength to go on
Giving up a little strength brings relief

7♥ – TECHNOLOGY

CHARACTER

Role/Pursuit: analyst, android, chemist, computer whiz, engineer, entrepreneur, factory worker, geek, genius, hacker, information broker, inventor, lab technician, Luddite, mad scientist, research scientist, robot, software designer statistician, survivalist, tinker, visionary

Trait: intelligent, forward-thinking, imaginative, curious, inquisitive, focused, logical, objective, rational, highbrow, introverted, nerdy, skeptical, anti-technology, emotionless, uncaring, irrational

Goal/Motivation:
Find a technological solution to handle a problem
Make a new product work
Get funding or approval for your new idea/invention
Escape from technology and live off the grid
Destroy the technology that is making your life miserable

Internal Conflict:
Fear of a new technology hampers your ability to succeed
Lacking empathy
Unable to think rationally about an objective
Too focused on the outcome to see the steps needed to get there
Lacking scientific knowhow to make your idea work

External Conflict:
A new technology threatens your livelihood
A new invention threatens apocalypse
Someone steals your idea
Destruction of an invention or technology hinders your progress
The technology you revere causes many problems

Growth/Realization:
Technology is not the answer—you are
Embracing technology leads to happiness
Reliance on technology is dangerous
Giving up technology is freeing
People are as important as technology

PLOT

Ordinary World:
Living in a high-tech environment or dependent on machines
Living off the grid
Totally dependent on machines
Living in a post-apocalyptic world without technology
The victim of technological experiments

Trigger Event/Change of Plans:
A new invention changes everything
Destruction of technology is devastating
Technology doesn't work as planned

A scientist/inventor upsets your plans
A hacker ruins your life

Black Moment:

Technology fails when you need it most
Must choose between a person or your idea
Implementation of your idea/invention threatens chaos
The technology/invention is too strong to overcome
The technology you need is not available

Resolution:

Using a new invention helps you to succeed
Removing/Destroying technology brings victory
You are celebrated for your contribution to the world
Working with technology instead of against it brings success
Giving up on a technological solution brings a different kind of achievement

8♥ – TIME

CHARACTER

Role/Pursuit: Angler, antiquarian, antique dealer, archeologist, astronomer, clock maker, death row inmate, farmer, forecaster, fortune teller, futurist, genealogist, gerontologist, historian, immortal being, indentured servant, Methuselah, paleontologist, racer, savings bond holder, senior citizen, timekeeper, time traveler

Trait: Punctual, efficient, effective, old-fashioned, swift, ageless, precocious, deliberate, busy, regular, psychic, mature, youthful, elderly, archaic, long-lived, procrastinating, unfocused, primitive, slow, wasteful, hasty, tardy, squandering, dilatory, terminally ill

Goal/Motivation:
Halt the passage of time
Take time out
Predict the future
Learn what happened in the past
Find a piece of history

Internal Conflict:

Always running late

There aren't enough hours in the day

Time hangs heavy on your hands

You want to procrastinate

Afraid of what the future will bring

External Conflict:

Time is running out

You are considered too old

History threatens to repeat itself

You have no future and/or past

You can't perform fast enough to please another

Growth/Realization:

Time heals all wounds

Lost time is never found again

There must be a first time for everything

There's no time like the present

Many people will forget the past for a present

PLOT

Ordinary World:

Living on borrowed time

Studying the past

Predicting the future

Your life runs as regular as clockwork

Never have enough time

Trigger Event/Change of Plans:

You are given a time limit

History repeats itself

You receive a prediction about your future

You are suddenly left with too much time on your hands
You learn you have only months left to live

Black Moment:

Time has run out
There is no future for you
You are condemned to repeat the past
You have nothing left but time
You are too late

Resolution:

Making time for others brings happiness
Reassessing priorities gives you time to succeed
Being late is a blessing in disguise
Learning from the mistakes of the past helps you succeed in the present
Making the right decision helps you plan for the future

9♥ – TRAVEL

CHARACTER

Role/Pursuit: Adventurer, ambassador, astronaut, bounty hunter, cab driver, castaway, circus performer, explorer, free spirit, fugitive, guide, gypsy, hiker, homebody, hotelier, mercenary, migrant, nomad, orator, pilot, prisoner, questor, sailor, scuba diver, sky diver, stay-at-home, tinker, tourist, travel agent, traveling salesman, truck driver, vagabond, wanderer, yachtsman

Trait: Nomadic, curious, adventurous, questing, eager, bold, courageous, enterprising, mobile, footloose, changeable, unsettled, rootless, driven, obsessed, restless, bored, tied down, scared, impatient, weary, dissatisfied, lost, edgy, immobile

Goal/Motivation:
Travel and see the world
Never have to travel again
Find roots
Help others move on

See what's on the next horizon

Internal Conflict:
You want to move on
You have no roots
Tired of traveling
Too restless to stay in one place
Runs with scissors

External Conflict:
You are too far away
You are forced to travel elsewhere
Can't afford to travel
Travel is forbidden or restricted
You are forced to pull up roots and move on

Growth/Realization:
You travel faster when you travel alone
A traveler never gets lost on a straight road
Travel broadens your horizons
Putting down roots is the only way to grow
It's harder to hit a moving target

PLOT

Ordinary World:
Leading a nomadic existence
You are bound to one location
Working in the travel business
Working toward a special trip
Always on the move

Trigger Event/Change of Plans:
An unexpected trip becomes necessary

You are uprooted
Your travel plans go awry
A mysterious traveler comes into your life
You win a free trip

Black Moment:

You are stuck in one place forever
Your decision causes a people's diaspora
You are forced to wander for the rest of your life
Your roots shrivel up and die
You are unable to move

Resolution:

Settling down brings peace of mind
Success frees you to travel
Moving on brings relief
Pulling up roots widens your horizons
Helping others move on brings satisfaction

10♥ – UNKNOWN

CHARACTER

Role/Pursuit: Alien, channeler, creator, cultist, debunker, deity, fakir, futurist, ghost hunter, inventor, investigator, monster, phantom, psychic, researcher, seer, spirit, spiritual being, spy, telekinetic, visionary

Trait: Spiritual, psychic, sensitive, imaginative, intuitive, inventive, telepathic, mysterious, hopeful, fey, perceptive, creative, devout, metaphysical, mystical, unearthly, supernatural, superhuman, unknowable, unknowing

Goal/Motivation:
Explore the unknown
Guard the secrets of the unknown
Obtain assistance from the unknown
Make the unknown known
Ensure you are no longer unknown

Internal Conflict:
Fear of the unknown
Don't know how to proceed
Don't know how to use your own abilities
Don't believe in the unknown
Relying too much on the help of unknown forces

External Conflict:
Unknown forces are opposing you
You are an unknown quantity to others
Can't penetrate the secrets of the unknown
You don't know why things are happening to you
Forces from the unknown refuse to help you

Growth/Realization:
To be unknown is better than to be ill known
What is unknown is unmissed
Some mysteries are better left unexplained
No one knows what will happen next
You never know what you can do until you try

PLOT

Ordinary World:
Constantly seeking evidence of the unknown
Unknown and forgotten in the world
Bringing an unknown from obscurity into the light
Helping others discover and reach the unknown
Working with unknown forces

Trigger Event/Change of Plans:
An unexpected natural disaster occurs
The unknown suddenly becomes known
You discover you have power over the unknown

The unknown suddenly affects you
Unknown forces turn your world upside down

Black Moment:
The path to success is unknown to you
You can't fight unknown forces
Revealing the unknown is life-threatening
Can't penetrate the unknown
You don't know enough to proceed

Resolution:
Leaving the unknown alone brings peace
Revealing the unknown brings success
The unknown becomes known, bringing relief
Believing in the unknown brings wisdom
Remaining unknown and obscure is the best solution

J🤍 – WAR

CHARACTER

Role/Pursuit: Aggressor, barbarian, berserker, brawler, camp follower, contestant, defender, dissident, draftee, fencer, fighter, genocide, gun runner, invader, medic, mercenary, military dependent, officer, peacemaker, prisoner of war, rebel, resistance fighter, rival, sailor, soldier, strategist, tactician, terrorist, traitor, usurper, war survivor, war widow, warrior

Trait: Patriotic, brave, valiant, honorable, gutsy, bold, heroic, fearless, plucky, loyal, disciplined, defensive, homesick, scared, belligerent, fearsome, aggressive, savage, ferocious, combative, predatory, militant, cornered, hostile, crippled, careless, pugnacious, cruel, barbarous, hedonistic, destructive, divisive, quarrelsome, hostile, inhumane

Goal/Motivation:
Survive a war
Prevent or stop a war

Fight for what you believe in
Defend yourself against an aggressor
Profit from a war

Internal Conflict:
Unable to choose sides in a war
Want to avoid conflict at all costs
Combative attitude gets you in trouble
You are a coward
Can't find peace

External Conflict:
You are losing the battle
Unable to defend yourself
Can't escape the fighting
Invaders threaten your way of life
You are forced to choose sides

Growth/Realization:
The fiercest opponent is the one who has nothing to lose
Never underestimate your opponent
Don't fight a losing battle
War is hell
The object of war is peace

PLOT

Ordinary World:
Living in a war-torn society
Living the military life
Seeking peace
Continually terrorized
Fighting for what you believe in

Trigger Event/Change of Plans:
Your country declares war
A fight is forced upon you
War is suddenly over
Terrorists attack
You declare war on another

Black Moment:
The war is lost
Continuing to fight will bring untold devastation
Winning a war means losing your self-respect
Peace is shattered
Giving in to a terrorist opens the way to more terrorization

Resolution:
The war is over and you find peace at last
Refusing to fight brings self-respect
Fighting for what you believe in brings success
Losing a fight isn't as devastating as you feared
Winning a fight brings satisfaction

Q♥ – WISDOM

CHARACTER

Role/Pursuit: Academic, adept, ancestor, authority, crone, dunce, egghead, elder, expert, forefather, genius, graduate, guru, idiot, intellectual, mentor, oracle, parent, philosopher, pundit, ruler, sage, savant, scholar, scientist, swami, theorist, wise one

Trait: Wise, peaceful, civilized, knowledgeable, sharp, logical, educable, experienced, decisive, educated, diplomatic, cultured, ivory-towerish, enlightened, respected, erudite, rational, ignorant, hardheaded, illiterate, know-it-all, closed-minded, stupid, boastful

Goal/Motivation:
Gain wisdom
Obtain the wisdom of another
Pass your wisdom on to another
Become wise in the ways of the world
Choose wisely

Internal Conflict:
You lack wisdom
You fear being considered a fool
Desire wars with wisdom
Wisdom is a millstone around your neck
You fear making an unwise decision

External Conflict:
Your wisdom is challenged
Others make you look foolish
Others are far wiser than you
A wise one challenges you
Wisdom is dangerous

Growth/Realization:
Wisdom doesn't always speak in Greek and Latin
Authority without wisdom is like a heavy axe without an edge
Understanding is the beginning of wisdom
A wise man changes his mind; a fool never does
The wise person says it cannot be done; the fool does it

PLOT

Ordinary World:
Considered the fount of all wisdom
Seeking wisdom
Trying to enlighten those around you
Being foolish
Surrounded by those wiser than you

Trigger Event/Change of Plans:
An unwise decision comes back to haunt you
The sudden acquisition of wisdom changes everything
You decide to seek a sage's advice

You realize how unwise you have been
You ignore common wisdom

Black Moment:

Your foolishness brings disaster
You are revealed to be a fool
There is no wisdom in your choice
Others are proven far wiser than you
An unwise choice proves devastating

Resolution:

Making the right choice brings wisdom
Practicing wisdom brings success
Losing brings wisdom
Ignoring common wisdom allows you to overcome failure
Overcoming foolishness brings reward

K♥ – ZENITH

CHARACTER

Role/Pursuit: Boss, CEO, champion, chess master, chief, conqueror, diva, empress, failure, fashion leader, finisher, first lady, gang leader, general, head honcho, high society, legend, loser, master, mastermind, mountain climber, Olympic medalist, president, quitter, royalty, social climber, star, trendsetter, victor, winner

Trait: Confident, skilled, competent, fashionable, ambitious, successful, accomplished, focused, determined, majestic, secure, content, driven, detached, regal, dedicated, commanding, goal-oriented, powerful, stubborn, unbending, unscrupulous, domineering, elitist, ruthless

Goal/Motivation:
Be at the top of your profession
Reach the peak
Be all you can be
Find success

Topple someone from their high position

Internal Conflict:
You hate being second best
Don't want to be on top
Maintaining your top position is wearying
You are ashamed of your ambitions
Success brings nothing but pain

External Conflict:
You haven't reached the peak yet
Your goal is out of reach
Others are better than you
Someone is trying to topple you from your heights
Your accomplishments are sneered at

Growth/Realization:
It's lonely at the top
If at first you don't succeed, try, try again
To achieve success, you must earn it
Success often costs more than it is worth
The cream of the crop will rise to the top

PLOT

Ordinary World:
You are a living legend
Constantly striving to reach the top
At the top of your profession
Helping others reach their potential
Pretending to be the top dog in your profession

Trigger Event/Change of Plans:
Someone beats you

You finally reach the top
The top is suddenly within reach
You fall from the top
The bar is raised too high

Black Moment:
You reach the zenith to find nothing there
You realize you will never reach the top
There's nowhere to go but down
Achieving the zenith brings nothing but problems
Being on top harms others

Resolution:
Reaching the top brings satisfaction
Fulfilling your full potential brings success
The struggle to succeed is more rewarding than the success itself
Settling for second best brings relief
The end of your ambition brings gratitude

ABOUT THE AUTHORS

Pam McCutcheon

After many years of working for the military as enlisted, officer and civil service successively, Pam McCutcheon left her industrial engineering position to pursue her first love—a career in publishing. Luckily, the synthesis of these two disparate careers hasn't made her schizophrenic, but instead has given her an unusual combination of logic and creativity and the ability to speak from both sides of her brain. She has put these to use in developing writing classes and in writing two books for writers, including *Writing the Fiction Synopsis: A Step by Step Approach* and the book you hold in your hand.

Fond of incorporating humor in her books and classes, Pam is an award-winning author of romantic comedy, paranormal romance, and fantasy short stories under her own name, and urban fantasy under the name Parker Blue. She can be found in beautiful Colorado Springs with her rescue dogs or on the Internet at PamMc.com.

Michael Waite

Michael is the principal of Bonefrog Creative, and has developed a multifaceted expertise in marketing, design and business communications. After some ten years of working for design shops, an ad agency, and a magazine, Michael opened his own creative shop in 1994 and chased the projects that challenged and intrigued him—where ever they were found. He writes extensively for clients in a diverse collection of business arenas and lives in a quite rural valley in southeast Idaho with his wife, a huntin' cat, and a small herd of Macs.

www.ingramcontent.com/pod-product-compliance
Lightning Source LLC
Chambersburg PA
CBHW071022280326
41935CB00011B/1454